Igniting the Power to Succeed

T. R. Williams

Igniting the Power to Succeed.

SECOND EDITION
Printed on acid-free paper

Library of Congress Cataloging-in-Publication Data
has been applied for.

1. Success in Business 2. Self-improvement
3. Inspirational/ Motivational Quotes

ISBN 0-9718620-0-1

Layout and Cover design by
Estell Jaxxon

Rōz & Company
P. O. Box 2097
Missouri City, TX 77459
(281) 499-5012

Igniting the Power to Succeed is available at special quantity discounts for bulk purchases for sales promotions, premiums, fund raising or educational use.

For more details contact
Eagles Wings Inc.
1749 Texas Parkway, Suite 180
Houston-Missouri City, Texas 77489
www.eagleswingsinc.com
e-mail: trwilliams@eagleswingsinc.com

Acknowledgements

To my wife, Shunta Renee, thank you for sticking by my side during the lean years, during the frustrating and disappointing days and the happy times in between. I had no idea we would have to go through so much before our season of harvest arrived. God is faithful and so are you. You *are* my good and perfect gift.

To my parents, Robbie Evans and Levi Williams Jr., thank you for loving me unconditionally and instilling in me the desire to succeed. You are a continuous source of encouragement. I'm proud of you, and I know the feeling is mutual.

To the Drs. I.V. and Bridgett Hilliard, words cannot express the debt of gratitude I owe you. My life *is* better after having heard the Word of Faith.

To Dr. Myles Munroe, I can't count the messages that have kept me on course to understanding my purpose and releasing my potential. Thank you for understanding your purpose and releasing your potential.

To Jack Canfield and Brian Tracy, thank you for illuminating and expanding my understanding of methods for experiencing peak performance and personal fulfillment.

To Rosie Blaylock, Erik and Cindy Cork, Dennis Brown, Keith Harrell, Carla Holmes, Margaret Evans, Lee Mashburn, David Evans, Ivy Lopez , Bernadette Richardson-Gueary, Nancy Johnson, Estell Jaxxon, Marie Hampton, Elder Ron and Sis. Jeorgia Eagleton your encouragement and assistance have been the wind beneath my wings.

The Dedication

To the countless number of people who have significantly influenced my life, I pause to say "thank you". With each encouraging word, admonishment, caution and rebuke you have helped me become the man I am. Writing this book has made me realize how blessed I am to have so many incredible people enhance my life.

And finally to the Alpha and Omega, the author and finisher of my faith, my Saviour and Lord Jesus Christ. To the One who is and is to come, I offer my life, talents, abilities, dreams and ambitions for your glory. Thank you for paying the price so that I could experience abundant living in this life and the one to come.

Contents

The Summary

If you want to earn more, learn more, achieve more, receive more, give more and live more, THIS BOOK IS FOR YOU. This book was written for those who want to move to the next level of achievement, maximized performance, financial prosperity and personal fulfillment.

The fact that you have invested in yourself by purchasing ***Igniting the Power to Succeed*** indicates that you desire a greater level of success in life, the workplace, or the classroom. You want to experience the full abundance that life has to offer.

The life-transforming lessons in this book are based on proven principles. They have transformed the lives of millions of people around the world including author and speaker T. R. Williams. They are not mere figments of the imagination. They are rock solid, tried and true approaches to life's situations. They are universally applicable life-changing lessons, if you practice these practical lessons they will change your life and your future forever.

The Message

At periodic points on the journey to our destiny, we face road blocks, unforeseen challenges, mental burnout, and frustration by the cares of life. I believe we all want a formula or strategy for getting past the tar pits of life. We want a method for leaping over the hurdles in the race of life. We want to succeed. The power to succeed is within every person. The frustrating challenge is how to ignite the power and ability to succeed at critical points in life.

Just as there are formulas that we use in algebra, calculus or physics, there are formulas for achieving success. Just as there are principles that are used in management, marketing and sales, there are principles for maximizing potential and experiencing fulfillment.

Unfortunately, most success principles are not taught in our schools, colleges or universities. In the workplace more time is spent planning the Christmas party than training every employee how to use their abilities and skills to benefit the company, themselves, and their families.

For the past twenty years, I have taken deliberate action on a daily basis to transform my life so that I could release the potential inside me. You don't have to take twenty years to experience your transformation. I have condensed the essential elements that transformed my life in this book. Learn from my experience and the experiences of other experts and professionals in varying fields of development and achievement. Use this book to catapult yourself into a bigger, brighter more productive future.

The Mission

My mission is to liberate individuals from small thinking to maximize their potential and then show them step-by-step how to set goals and then exceed them and enjoy doing it.

My passion and goal is to develop a superior group of executives, managers, educators, employees, parents and students who are well trained to lead and manage effectively while experiencing successful and fulfilling lives. I can show you how to move from where you are to where you want to be.

The Method

To receive the maximum benefit from this tool for transformation, read a chapter twice daily. The goal is not to complete the book quickly. The goal is to learn each lesson well and take action on what you have learned. Reserve one of your readings for the quiet time at night just before retiring to bed.

Be committed to completing the short assignments in each chapter. Doing so will help speed your transformation. Remember, to experience the maximum impact follow the directions completely and watch the amazing transformation.

The fuel that ignites the power to succeed is your desire for change in your life. Never lay aside your desire to change. Guard it at all costs. Your desire to change is your passport to a brighter, productive and prosperous future.

How Will You Profit From Reading This Book

Igniting the Power to Succeed is packed with practical performance methods for achieving phenomenal results. Every lesson is filled with universal principles, strategies, tools and practical points that will empower you to release the power of your potential. This book is a condensed, no non-sense, to-the-point guide for experiencing maximized performance, academic achievement, professional advancement, and personal fulfillment.

There are over **400** power points, positive thoughts, quotes, affirmations, analogies, tools, strategies, and real-life stories. Every life-changing principle is accompanied by illuminating examples. You will learn the practical application of each principle and practical strategies for specific circumstances and challenges in life. Here is how you will profit from reading this book; it will reveal how you can…

Igniting the Power to Succeed

T. R. Williams

Success

"To laugh often and much;
to win the respect of intelligent people
and the affection of children;
to earn the appreciation of honest critics
and endure the betrayal of false friends;
to appreciate beauty, to find the best in others;
to leave the world a bit better,
whether by a healthy child,
a garden patch or a redeemed social condition;
to know even one life has breathed easier
because you have lived. This is to have succeeded."

Ralph Waldo Emerson
Writer/Poet

Today and every day I take personal responsibility for believing, achieving and receiving the abundance that life has to offer.

Lesson One:

Preparing Your Mind for Success

I had a full day ahead of me. I was scheduled to speak to over 2000 students on Successful Test Taking Strategies and 7 Habits of Highly Effective Achievers and that evening I was presenting an *Igniting the Power to Succeed* ™ seminar for parents. Allen Poynter, the Youth Services Coordinator, picked me up at the hotel at 8:00 a. m. and it was off to the schools in Glasgow, Kentucky.

It was a beautiful morning, the sun was shining and bright yellow daffodils dotted the rolling green hills. Our first stop was Barron County Middle School. The building was located on a picturesque hillside overlooking a small stream. As I was escorted into the building, I immediately noticed how orderly the students were and how well kept the building was. I instantly knew that this was a place that was conducive to learning. There were banners on the walls and motivational sayings along with numerous academic accolades for state and national recognition for academic excellence.

I was introduced to the principal Ms. Michelle Pedigo. She had a forlorn countenance as she shook my hand and said "Mr. Williams I apologize if I seem a little frazzled around the edges, but last night one of my students passed away. It was an unexpected death and we are all trying to deal with it. This is the first student to die in the history of our school, and many students are shocked."

She continued, "I know we have invited you to help our kids with their academics and life skills, but I don't know if they are going to be in the right state of mind to benefit from all you have to offer." I told her not to worry and that I was sure that it was no accident that I had arrived on the day of such tragic news. I asked Allen to take me to the cafeteria. I requested a pair of latex rubber gloves from one of the food service workers and I was ready to begin the day. As we walked down to the assembly Allen asked, "What are you going to do with those gloves?" I told him I was going to use a pair of latex gloves to turn a sad day into a glad day.

As the students began to file in, I mentally began to create a completely new presentation for the students. My thoughts began to flow like the water in the stream outside the school. They were clear and precise and I had no hesitation about making this on-the-spot transition. My level of enthusiasm grew as the number of students increased. By the time I was introduced I was powered up and ready to transform their emotions, attitudes, and their lives.

My presentation was a tremendous success. The kids left informed, excited, and telling each other to have a "Super Fantastic Day." The entire atmosphere of the school had changed. Ms. Pedigo came up to me and said "I don't believe what I saw happen here. You were right, it was not an accident that you are here today."

As I left the school, I began to reminisce about how much my life had changed from being the person I used to be to the person I am today. As a struggling student I could have never dreamed I could transform the lives of people around the world. My life story is about transformation. I know what it means to experience failure and success. Believe me success is better!

I believe success and fulfillment are not restricted to those who are smart or to those who have great abilities and talents. It is not restricted to those who have outgoing personalities and Madison Avenue profiles. Success and fulfillment are not restricted to those who are rich or to those who live on the right side of town. It is not restricted by age, sex, race, or education. However, success is reserved for a special group of individuals, an uncommon group of individuals. Success is reserved for those who are willing to do what it takes to be successful.

Achievement, advancement, and fulfillment are determined by desire, motivation, consistency, and persistence. Doing what it takes to go the extra mile, even when you are exhausted. To take the initiative to make a difference with your life. To think creatively, to break out of the box of traditionalism, to dare to dream the impossible dream. To leave the crowd and stand alone, knowing that those who break barriers and create new paths often do so without the applause or approval of the crowd.

In the following twelve simple lessons, I will share practical proven principles that are life transforming. As you practice the lessons in this book they will positively change your life, family, organization, business or students. Allow me to share how my journey for success and fulfillment began and then we will begin our first lesson on your journey to a new level of bigger thinking, higher achievement, and dynamic living.

I grew up 17 miles east of Houston, Texas in the small town of Crosby. Everyone knew each other and I enjoyed the small, country town environment. We lived in a middle class community and I always felt safe in our home on Red Oak Drive.

For years my father taught carpentry, math, and science at the local junior and senior high schools. He enjoyed building furniture and remodeling homes. My mother was a hospital administrator at Ben Taub Hospital in Houston. After working her way through the ranks she was promoted to Vice President of Nursing. She was responsible for managing over 500 nurses providing care to patients.

Both my parents had come from humble backgrounds and through diligence and hard work were able to provide a comfortable life for themselves and their children. They taught us that hard work and a commitment to being the best was the path to success and happiness.

As a child I always knew that I had great potential. I knew that there was an unexplainable desire and drive to make my life count and to be an instrument of positive change. The challenge and quest during my formative years was how to release my potential so that I could achieve my goals and dreams.

The first four years of elementary school were fun-filled years, and I excelled in class and loved school. However, my problems began when the academic challenges of the fifth grade took the joy out of school as I began to struggle in math.

I was completely confused in my math class. Every day I had to sit in the class and feel like I was not as smart as the other students. Somewhere I had missed some math concepts and I had no idea how to go back and retrieve them. The other kids were getting the information. I knew that math could not be that hard to understand. Every time I entered my math class, I could feel the anxiety and the weight of feeling inferior cover me like a wet blanket.

My dad tried to help me, but subconsciously I was developing a mental block to receiving new information about math. I was convincing myself that I was not as smart as the other students, and my terrible test scores were a testament to my beliefs.

I was placed in a remedial class where I could get help with math. Although the teachers and my parents did the best they could, the damage had been done and for the next seven years in every class where mathematical concepts were presented, I struggled like a drowning man going down for the last time. My fear and failure in math negatively impacted my view of who I was and what I could accomplish.

I began to believe that I wasn't good enough based on the high standards I had set for myself. I always wanted to be the best. Mediocrity was never an expectable option. My parents instilled in me a desire for excellence. I wanted to be a straight A student, but I struggled to earn a B average. I wanted to be tall and muscular like my three brothers; I was stuck being short and thin. I wanted to be outgoing and confident, but deep inside I was insecure.

I tried to mask my insecurities by getting involved in numerous school and community activities. I was in the band, the speech club, the school newspaper club, the community newspaper staff, the drama club, student council, the student Red Cross club. Additionally I was in the church choir, little league baseball and football, the tennis team, statistician for the basketball team, and on and on. I thought that by getting involved and pleasing others, I could find fulfillment so I did everything I could to please my parents, my teachers and most of my friends. This lead to a strong need to have the approval of others to gain a sense of self-worth.

I internalized most of my feelings, frustrations and fears. On the outside I looked and acted like the model student while on the inside I was unsatisfied. I had to find a way to become the person I wanted to be and break free from the opinions and expectations of others.

It was during my junior year in high school that I began to make a conscious effort to break free from the chains of low self-esteem and unrealized potential. I began to read books about people who had experienced success. I found that they all had a unwavering belief or faith that success was possible for them.

Every successful person I studied followed his own dream and course in life. I soon realized that I had to change my outlook on life. I had to take personal responsibility for my own future. I started my transformation by getting my thoughts and beliefs aligned with *my* dreams and *my* desires. I learned that despite my past failures, I could be successful and experience personal fulfillment, but it was up to me to make the change.

I had to recondition my mind for success. Years of doubt, insecurity, and failure had conditioned me to expect more of the same. If I was going to experience fulfillment, I would have to recondition my mind to expect to experience success. For the next twenty years I was engaged in a self-imposed program of maximizing my mental, spiritual and physical development.

In this chapter you will learn how to recondition your mind to experience any level of success you desire. You will learn how to develop a can-do mentality and discard the can't-do mentality. The process of transformation begins in the mind of an individual.

When you truly believe you can succeed, amazingly, your mind will always discover a way and the means to make success happen. However, you must believe it before your can achieve it. **Believing in yourself is the single most important ingredient to experience life-long success.**

Condition the Soil for the Harvest

When I was a child, I had the privilege of spending the summers and holidays with my grandparents. They lived on a small farm on the banks of the Brazos River in the small town of Rosharon, Texas. They grew all types of vegetables. I learned many valuable life lessons on their farm. My grandfather taught me an important lesson regarding planting seeds and reaping a harvest.

Before my grandfather planted vegetable seeds, he would always till the soil, pull out the weeds and add natural fertilizer to the ground. He understood that if he wanted to reap the maximum harvest, he had to prepare the ground properly to receive the seeds he planted. My grandfather recognized that planting seeds in unprepared soil would never yield a satisfactory harvest.

Your mind is like the earth. It must be prepared for the seeds of success you will be planting. The first step to transforming your present situation is to take the time, energy and calculated effort to understand how your mind functions. Then you must prepare your mind for the life transforming information you will learn and experience as you walk through the pages of this book. **Your mind is the soil from which a bountiful new crop of possibilities will emerge.**

Your thoughts are the seeds that will yield a harvest for your future. We are the products of our own thoughts. **The thoughts of your mind are the flames that will ignite your personal power to succeed. Your thoughts and beliefs can also be fountains of hopelessness and despair that extinguish your potential and drown your possibilities.** Thoughts have power. Thoughts are energy and you can make your world or destroy it by your own thinking. What you believe about who you are, what you can do, what you can have, and where you can go all impact your ability to succeed in life.

Doubt is the combustible fuel of the power to fail. When you doubt your ability to succeed, your mind automatically produces countless reasons to justify the disbelief. It is only when you see yourself as a winner and not a loser that you can overcome doubt. **Understanding who you are is the key that will free you from lower level thinking, lower level behavior, lower level expectations and lower level living.**

Reconditioning Your Mind

Your mind is an incredibly creative organ. It is the mental power source for the achievement of what your mind believes or imagines. You may have heard it said that "If you can believe it, you can achieve it." Your transformation into a bigger thinker and higher achiever must first begin by reconditioning your mind for success. The most valuable resource you posses is your mind. **The power of your mind is so vast that once you discover its ability, it is incredible what you can achieve.** The information in this section may seem abstract, but it is essential that you understand it.

Let us look at how your mind is designed to function. Just as your brain is separated into two halves, known as the right brain and the left brain, your mind is also separated into two halves, known as the conscious mind and the subconscious mind or subconscious awareness. The conscious mind is the logical, decision-making control center. The subconscious mind is the repository of all the beliefs that govern how you respond to everything around you.

All systematic or methodical reasoning is processed in the conscious mind. It has the ability to accept or reject information. Once the conscious mind has analyzed, processed and accepted information, it transmits the information to the subconscious mind, which then sets the boundaries for beliefs, behavior, and performance. Most learning takes place in the conscious mind. Proficiency and mastery occur when the information learned is transferred to the subconscious.

That is why you can recall your telephone number without having to look it up in the phone book, or why you can add in your head without counting your fingers. The subconscious enables a musician to play a musical instrument without looking at the fingering positions for each note every time he plays. The fingers are automatically directed without conscious thought. **Your subconscious is a tool for creating change in your life once it is programmed for bigger thinking and enhanced performance.**

Anything you have ever thought or experienced is permanently stored in your subconscious. Your subconscious serves as the brain's memory bank. People who go through near-death experiences often report that their whole life passes before them. They see people and events from their past.

This is possible because the information has been stored in their brains. A catastrophic event or even hypnosis can jog the subconscious mind into releasing memories to the conscious.

Your subconscious also serves as the brain's command center. The subconscious awareness is always active, alert and is processing information, even while you sleep. It receives information from your conscious mind without question. Your subconscious does what it is told. It is the loyal servant of the conscious mind. It takes instruction and executes commands based on stored information.

The subconscious mind has infinite storage capacity for all the information you deposit into it. Once the information is stored in your subconscious mind you don't have to re-learn things. Your subconscious can provide perfect recall and instant response with very little conscious effort.

Your conscious mind is constantly processing information from many different sources and determining what to accept and what to reject. The information that is in agreement with your subconscious will be accepted while new information that is in opposition to your subconscious beliefs will be rejected. Without the coordination from the subconscious mind, you will be hindered in making good decisions that lead to maximum productivity and purposeful living.

This is why it is critical that you embark on a daily exercise of reconditioning your mind for success. You must feed your mind new information based on what you want to materialize. This can be rejuvenating as you consistently focus on new possibilities.

By doing this you will put your mind on cruise control as you travel to your brighter future. **The systematic reprogramming of the subconscious mind will yield infinite rewards.**

Five ways to daily enhance the use of the subconscious awareness.

1. **A lifetime of information and experiences are yours for the asking.** Practice requesting your subconscious to retrieve specific information so you can use it to your benefit.

2. **Your subconscious mind responds to stimulation.** Provide a constant diet of information that is educational, motivational, and emotionally stimulating to move to the next level of success and purposeful living.

3. **Your subconscious mind does not know the difference between that which is real and that which is imagined.** Imagine yourself achieving your dreams and desires.

4. **Use your subconscious as an aid to solve your problems and create new ideas.** Your subconscious is your servant. Before going to bed pray for an answer or idea, then be prepared to receive the answer.

5. **Always be prepared for inspiration and answers to come, and write them down.** There is no warning before inspiration comes, so always have a pad, pen, or recorder nearby so that you can quickly retain your thoughts.

By following these directions for reconditioning the subconscious mind, you will begin to receive new ideas and increased motivation. You will begin to experience results, and your level of faith, enthusiasm, and commitment to the process will increase. Maximizing your mental abilities will make a significant change in what will materialize for you.

Some People Are Chosen

We will begin by learning methods for reconditioning your mind from being failure focused to being success focused. You may have been conditioned to think that success is very elusive and only a special or lucky class of people will be successful. **The systematic reprogramming of the subconscious mind will yield infinite rewards through changing your thinking.**

Many people embrace the idea that some people are successful because they were lucky. Luck will never produce life-long success. Gambling casinos make multi-millions of dollars on people who are depending on luck. Most people leave the casinos with less money than they had when they arrived. People who depend on luck usually end up on the losing end.

You may have heard it said that "Your future is outside your control because "God" is in control. He has chosen some people to be rich and others to be poor. Forget those dreams, forget improving your grades, forget succeeding in business, forget that larger home, forget going to college, forget a better life, because if God wanted you to have those things, He would have automatically given them to you." I want to caution you, do not listen to the voices of lack, limitation, and failure.

Don't accept this misconception. This type of fatalistic thinking must be uprooted, destroyed, and never be allowed to sow seeds of defeat in your mind again. Don't blame God or anyone else for your present situation or circumstances. The Bible is replete with passages that clearly state that those who diligently serve God should prosper and live an abundant life. **It's time you take personal responsibility for where you are in life and take responsibility for changing your circumstances.** The responsibility is yours.

I Was Born This Way

I am fully persuaded that every person wants to succeed. We all come into the world wanting the best this life has to offer. We were not created to spend our lives crawling around on our hands and knees. Normal human development requires that we begin to pull ourselves up and learn to stand erect and walk upright. We have to be conditioned to be content with living on the lower level in mediocrity. We have to be conditioned to believe we can't be successful. Therefore, many of us have to be reconditioned to believe we can be successful.

Thoughts of success and failure can never occupy the same space. Your brain becomes magnetized with the dominating thoughts which you allow to take root in your mind. You are drawn to the forces, the people, and the circumstances of life that will be in agreement with your strongest thoughts and beliefs. Before you can experience success financially, in business, in relationships or in any other area, you must become success conscious, even in the midst of a presently disappointing situation.

Diligently guard the thoughts that enter your mind. **Your continuous thoughts and deliberate actions will determine your future.** Self-defeating or negative thoughts are those thoughts that restrict you from wanting more, achieving more, and experiencing more out of life. They are like chains that restrict your freedom to move to the next level in life, in business, in your finances and in relationships.

You must develop an in-depth plan for how you will deal with self-defeating thoughts that will surely assault you during this time of transformation. Whenever a negative thought enters your mind, immediately reverse the thought to its positive counterpart.

For instance, if you decide that you are going to set you sights on improving your grades or improving your performance at work, a negative thought may be, "You can't change; you have been performing at a low level for so long, it will take forever to change. It's not worth the effort."

Your immediate response should be, "I have my whole future ahead of me, and the failures of my past will not hold me back from my fantastic future. I will do whatever it takes to succeed." **When a negative thought comes to your mind, don't nurse it, don't rehearse it, just quickly disburse it.**

It's time to pause and take action. During peaceful sleep your subconscious awareness functions at its maximum level of alertness and is open to receiving new information. This is the ideal time to add new positive information to counter the old thoughts of fear, failure, lack, mediocrity and lower level living.

Taking Action to Succeed

Reconditioning your mind to achieve peak performance and advancement requires deliberate action. Sometimes there are years of information and events stored in your subconscious that must be overcome. Use your sleep time to continue the process of using your subconscious as a partner in your progress. Starting tonight, before you fall asleep practice the following steps.

1. Lie flat on your back. Begin to relax every muscle beginning with your toes and work your way up until you are perfectly relaxed.

2. Focus your mind on having a full peaceful night's rest.

3. Repeat to yourself a positive thought expressing a positive desire (I can improve. I can succeed. I am smart. I am a winner. I am moving to a higher level of fulfillment. I will not worry because my faith is in God).

4. Just before falling to sleep imagine that you are receiving the answer for a fantastic idea or the answer or solution to a problem that is perplexing you.

By repeating this exercise nightly you will experience a deeper and more productive level of sleep. Your subconscious will be able to function at its maximum capacity. Be prepared to receive new ideas, answers to questions and a greater sense of direction as you sleep.

**"There are things that you were born to do
and things you were trained to do.
The secret to success and fulfillment
is to recognize the difference
and be bold enough to not allow
your training to deter you from doing
what you were born to do."**

T. R. Williams
Speaker/Author

Today and everyday
I will use my talents, skills and experience
to realize my full potential.

Lesson Two

Embrace Your Unique Purpose

We all want to feel that our lives are of value and that we can make a difference in the lives of others, at home or in the workplace. We want our lives to count. The search for significance is an endeavor that we all undertake throughout the course of our lives. To do this requires going through the continuing process of determining what brings you the greatest sense of joy and fulfillment. It is important to pinpoint the activities that evoke a peaceful, pleasing sensation deep within when you know your life and activities are making a difference. The internal desire to make a difference is connected to your sense of purpose.

Purpose is an internal desire, a passion, a driving force, a reoccurring calling to engage in specific activities, vocations, and causes that positively impact lives or the society in which you live. **Purpose inspires us to aim for powerful possibilities**. It elevates us above the mundane. Purpose provides clarity to dreams and goals. Purpose is the lifeline to fulfillment and a reason for living.

We are all born with a purpose. It is impossible to be born void of purpose. Just as the heart is essential to the proper functioning of the physical body, purpose is essential to experiencing a successfully fulfilling life. When you live life without a sense of your unique purpose, it leads to pursuing things that don't provide fulfillment when you have achieved or acquired them.

People lacking a sense of purpose live lives without direction and focus. **Navigating your way through life void of a sense of purpose is like sailing on the sea without a compass**.

Why Am I Here?

One of the most perplexing questions facing every person is the question, "Why am I here?" It is only when you can answer this question with confidence that you are able to pick the fruit of success from the tree of life and savor the sweet taste of personal fulfillment. Every individual should make a special contribution, during their life-time. It is a tragic thing to pass away without leaving your positive influence on those with whom you came in contact. However, it is up to each individual to understand what the contribution will be. To find the answer to this age-old question, consider another definition of purpose.

The purpose is the reason for which something exists or the maker's original intent for creating it. The Creator is the Master Designer. The manufacturer of the product determines its purpose and how the product or creation is designed to function. To find or understand your true purpose, consult the One who is your Master Designer. He is the giver of purpose.

Consider this point. The primary reason for manufacturing a product is there is a particular need or niche in the market place for that particular product. There is a specific use for which every product has been designed. When the product is used for the purpose for which it was designed, you get the maximum utilization from the product.

You were born with particular abilities and desires that correspond and equip you to fulfill your function or purpose. When you live your life and function according to your designed purpose, not only will you experience maximum fulfillment and productivity, you will also enhance the lives of countless others who come in contact with you.

As I travel across the country speaking, I am amazed at the vast number of young people who have never been told that they have a positive purpose in life. Many kids have never been told that the Master Creator has a unique role or purpose for them to fulfill. I am often asked the question, "Why is it so important that I develop my potential?" It is important to develop your potential because that is the path to discovering your purpose. **Your developed potential is the throttle that regulates the speed at which you begin to experience success and personal fulfillment.**

The One Who Really Matters

I am always cognizant that there is a sea of disheartened souls who have been poisoned by the venom of negative comments such as, "You are no good, you are an accident and I wish you were never born;" "You are dumb and stupid;" "You lazy bum, you'll never amount to anything;" "You are the wrong race; you are the wrong height. You are too fat; you are too thin. You are too ugly; you are too poor." We have all had to deal with negative comments that were spoken to tear us down, rather than lift us up. Sometimes words can hurt much worse than "sticks and stones." Negative words assault your soul and spirit and the healing process can take months and even years. Regrettably some people never recover.

To those who have suffered the slings and arrows of continuous verbal stabbing, I offer you a message from the Master Creator.

For I know the thoughts that I think toward you, says your God, thoughts of peace, and not of evil, I want to give you hope in a bright future. Jeremiah 29:11

It is so comforting to know that despite what others may think about you or what others say about you, the only One who really matters has clearly expressed His position. When you derive your identity from the Master Creator, then you will be free to experience the abundance that life has to offer. **The opinions of others should not influence you to doubt the Creator of the universe.**

I know that many times we place great value on how others view us. However, during this time of transformation, you must focus your attention on establishing your new identity based on the words and thoughts of the Master Creator. As you commit yourself to this endeavor, be assured that peace and a bright future await those who live according to their divine assignment known as purpose.

Your God given purpose is uniquely yours. No one can carry out your assignment like you can. We are all very different. We each have a unique way of doing what we do, looking like we look, and thinking like we think. Even identical twins have distinctions. During this time of transformation, unload any desires to be "just like" someone you have idealized. Don't get caught up in the comparison trap. Nurture your commitment to be the best "you" that is possible and embrace your unique purpose.

True success is *not* determined by your accomplishments compared to someone else's accomplishments. **True success is determined by assessing what you have done with your talents and abilities compared to what you were supposed to do with your talents and abilities.** Ultimate success is completing your divine purpose. When you focus on doing what you are supposed to do and spend less time trying to be carbon copies of other people you will experience greater fulfillment.

Please Use As Directed

Having a sense of purpose inspires higher achievement and enhanced performance. Knowledge of your purpose is the path to experience true success and fulfillment. When you don't know the purpose of something, you will create your own use or misuse for it. When you don't know your purpose, you will misuse time, energy and resources attempting to become someone you were never designed to be.

The misuse and abuse of human potential has wrapped its slimy tentacles around untold numbers of unsuspecting individuals and is sucking the life out of them. And many are not even aware of the peril of their desperate situations. When you don't know your purpose, it is difficult to live a fulfilling, successful life.

There are countless individuals who, despite achieving great fame and incredible fortunes, live lonely or empty lives because they don't have a sense of their divine purpose. **Success without fulfillment of purpose is a formula for emptiness of the soul.** Today, more than at any other time in history there are so many successful people suffering from emptiness of the soul.

Paths to Your Purpose

There are numerous paths to discover a stronger sense of purpose for your life. The revealing of purpose is a gradual process. At various stages and points in life, different aspects of purpose are revealed. There is no clear cut formula for realizing a sense of purpose. Purpose is an internal non-tangible asset. It is a mental or spiritual knowing that relies on intuition supported by corresponding action based on your personal beliefs.

Here are six common ways to discover a deeper sense of significance and purpose for your life.

1. **Spiritual Awakening** - Many individuals have gained a sense of purpose as a result of having a divine spiritual experience. They can point to a specific period or event in which they received a supernatural confirmation or instruction. Often they receive direction regarding what they should do with their talents and abilities.

2. **Progressive Revelation -** For some, the revealing of purpose is progressive, similar to Dorothy traveling down the yellow brick road in the story *The Wizard of Oz*. Through the course of her travels, Dorothy met key individuals at strategic points along the road to help her get to her destination. We all have people in our lives that influence and provide direction at important points in our lives. Sometimes we understand our purpose only after we look back over our life and see that there has been a reoccurring theme. This can provide direction and motivation for moving toward your purpose.

3. **An Internal Tug -** There are times and places in our lives when we begin to feel a strong internal tug to travel down a particular path or do a specific thing. For some it may mean seeking a promotion, starting a business or leaving one occupation and entering a different line of work. Still others find a sense of purpose in allowing their dormant creative and artistic talents to burst forth and flourish.

4. **A Passion -** For others purpose begins to exert its magnetic pull fostering a passion for engaging in a specific productive activity. For some individuals, these are years when their purpose in life will begin to influence their passions. Students should be encouraged to aggressively peruse their personal and vocational interests, while maintaining a commitment to academic excellence.

5. **A Special Attribute or Ability -** Everyone has talents and abilities, however some individuals have abilities that serve to direct their primary activities in life. Their enhanced talents or abilities allow them to distinguish themselves in specific fields and endeavors. Every tall person is not a basketball player. However, it is rare to find a successful professional basketball player that is short in height.

6. **A Call to Lead -** There comes a point in time when individuals gain a sense of purpose through assuming a leadership role. Some individuals are groomed for assuming leadership positions. Others faithfully function in the background until an event or circumstance catapults them in the leadership role. Once in the position they find renewed purpose, passion and vision.

Purpose and Profession

Purpose should not be confused with a profession. Sometimes your purpose may influence the profession you choose, but the two are very different. **Your purpose is your divine assignment in life.** Your profession is the field of employment by which you derive income. In many instances you can function according to your purpose in many different professions.

Your purpose may indicate that you could be well suited for a particular profession or organization. A strong connection between organizational and personal purpose can serve as the motivation for increased performance and fulfillment. Inspiration is fueled when individuals view their organization's purpose as an extension of their own personal purpose. Your profession could be a powerful vehicle to fulfill your divine purpose.

Consider this point. For individuals whose purpose in life is to help heal the sick, they may find fulfillment working in a large urban hospital or a small community clinic. Their desire to heal the sick may lead them to become a medical doctor, hospital administrator, or they may find fulfillment being a nurse or volunteering at a hospital. It is the internal desire to help others heal that is the thread that is woven through the tapestry of their lives.

Take time to examine your present condition regarding your profession and place of employment. In every organization there are individuals who seem plugged in and enjoy their work. However, there are scores of people who are just going through the motions in occupations or workplaces that live unfulfilled lives. They show up day after day doing just enough to get by.

Some are carrying out the dreams of their parents instead of their own dreams. Others were lured by the appeal of money or prestige but after a period of time begin to feel empty.

One summer afternoon, I was in a meeting with the regional manager of a national distribution company. We were going over the specifics of my training session on customer satisfaction, *How to Keep Them Coming Back for More.* Jeff was in his mid thirties. As we talked he began to share his personal dilemma. He had been attracted to a company by the lure of a $60,000 a year base salary and a generous incentive and benefits package.

After five years in the position, he was beginning to feel restrained. He was starting to ask, "Is there more to life?" He stated that he was no longer fulfilled coming to work day after day dealing with the same issues; he felt trapped. Jeff had gotten accustomed to his comfortable income. He felt he could not afford to take a cut in pay to do what he really wanted to do.

Jeff enjoyed being in the great outdoors. He found peace and contentment being surrounded by the beauty of nature. He wanted to get a job managing a resort in the mountains. Being in the office in a suit and tie every day was weighing heavy on him. He said that he felt like his life was slowly evaporating and that he would have nothing to show for it. The money and prestige were no longer enough to ignore the internal tug of his heart.

Search out ways to add greater meaning to your work and activities. Consider ways in which you could use your personal abilities, interests and passions to make a difference in the lives both inside and outside your workplace.

The ultimate impact of you fulfilling your purpose will be manifested in how you influence and impact individual lives in your sphere of influence and the society in which you live. This is why it is so important for you to find and fulfill your purpose. Others are in need of what you have to offer.

It's time to pause and take action. It's time to get the maximum benefit from the lesson. Give some serious thought to what your purpose may be. Is there an internal tug that won't wane? Is there a desire that you have deep in your being that repeatedly whispers, "Follow your heart?" Has there been an event that had such a strong impact on you that you knew from that moment what you had to do?

Taking Action to Succeed

Write down what you believe to be your mission or purpose in life. We will call this your *Purpose Statement*. Remember your purpose is not your profession. Purpose is the way you experience fulfillment while positively impacting others or the society in which you live. You will be better equipped to benefit from the next lesson when you complete this activity.

Do you know why you are here? ________________________

I believe my purpose in life is to________________________

____

____

____

Which path and events have lead you to your sense of purpose?

____

____

____

How are you fulfilling your purpose? ____________________

____

____

____

____

"Champions aren't made in gyms. Champions are made from something they have deep inside them a ...desire, a dream, a vision. They have to have last-minute stamina; they have to be a little faster. They have to have the skill and the will. But the will must be stronger than the skill"

Muhammad Ali
Boxing Legend

I will water my dreams and pull the weeds from around my ambitions so that my seeds of greatness will produce a bountiful harvest in my life.

Lesson Three

Igniting the Power of Your Potential

Everyone has incredible potential residing in them. The challenge facing all of us is how to get the unexposed talents, trapped ability, capped creativity, and our reserved power to become activated in our lives. When you are aware of your positive purpose and stand by that purpose, eventually it will become an all consuming obsession. The consuming obsession is what releases the power of potential.

A key element for experiencing success is having a clear purpose or a clear dream. Your clarity of purpose will empower you. In a matter of time your purpose or dream will have a life of its own when fueled by your consuming desire to see it materialize before your eyes.

Check Your Cable Connections

Consider this point. To start your car your battery cables must be properly connected to a charged battery. You are like a battery. A new battery contains all the power necessary to start the car's engine. However, if the battery cables are not properly connected, the power in the battery will not start the car and the vehicle will remain motionless. Even though all the equipment is in place, without the proper connection you can not reach your destination.

In you resides the power to achieve much more than you could ever imagine, but to benefit from the power of your potential, you must have a positive self-image. How you see yourself will determine what you choose to get out of life. It will also determine how others view you. **Your self-image is the battery cable to access the power of your potential.**

Building the Mind is like Building the Body

Each of us is born with exactly the same number of muscles in our bodies. As we mature, the muscles grow and our body shape begins to conform to the development of body tissue. There are some individuals called "body builders", who decide to develop their muscles to their maximum capacity. They are not content with allowing their bodies to remain in a moderate state of physical fitness. They are serious about maximizing their muscle potential.

Body builders develop a rigorous routine to maximize the development potential of every muscle in their bodies. They modify their diets, drink large amounts of water, and lift weights. As a result of their consistent and deliberate actions, their physical appearance is significantly different from the person who does not develop his muscles.

At this moment you have incredible potential lying dormant within you. To ignite the power of your potential, you must engage in a constant and deliberate series of exercises to maximize your potential, just as the body builder develops his muscles. **Always strive to become more than you are, if you want to become all that you can be.**

The body builder magazines regularly feature "before" and "after" pictures of individuals who have engaged in body building activities. Often it is difficult to recognize the person after months of exercise. They look totally different. In many cases they bear little physical resemblance to the person in the "before" picture. When you recognize the potential in you and begin to develop it, you will experience a remarkable transformation. Your "before" and "after" pictures will be very different.

From this point forward, never underestimate your potential. Use this book to develop your potential to its maximum capacity. You are the only person who can place limits on what you can achieve. **The sky is not the limit to your success. The moon, planets, sun, and stars await your arrival.**

The potential for success is already within you. To realize your potential requires a great deal of commitment and work. That is why many people don't get what they really want out of life. Being successful requires serious work. Those who are not committed will eventually get tired, get discouraged, get distracted, and will retreat back to their old ways of doing, thinking, and being.

Seeds of Success

At causal glance a corn seed is not impressive. A corn seed is a very small seed. The seed could easily be mistaken for a pebble. You've heard it said " you can't judge a book by its cover." It is also true that you can't judge the potential of a seed by its size. Be careful not to make a quick judgment based on appearance.

Incubating inside the small corn seed is everything needed for it to be all it was designed to become. **The contents of the seed determine its yield**. Inside the corn seed are roots. In the tiny corn seed is a stalk. Inside the seed are leaves. Inside the corn seed are four to six ears of corn. Inside one corn seed is an entire field of corn. All of the components of the corn plant have been encoded into the corn seed. The power in the seed is dormant until stimulated by the proper elements necessary for achieving its potential.

The encoded potential in the seed will remain in a state of dormancy until it is placed in an environment that is conducive to growth and maturity. The seed must be planted in fertile soil. The seed needs watering and requires the warmth of the sun's rays. When the corn seed is placed in an environment that is conducive to growth, something phenomenal begins to happen.

Internal changes begin to take place. The seed begins to absorb moisture from the soil and it begins to expand. In a matter of a few days, the tiny seed expands to the point that it splits open and small roots begin to reach beyond the confined boundaries of the seed.

The tiny roots begin to absorb life-strengthening nutrients from the soil, and growth is sustained. All of these changes are occurring beneath the surface. Even though the transformation has begun, it is not obvious to onlookers at the surface. **It is the internal transformation that will produce the external evidence of transformation.** Soon the tiny stem makes its exit from the seed and begins the process of pushing itself up through the soil. The seed has a natural ability to direct the roots to grow downward and to direct the stem to push upward.

The seed knows that to support the stalk and produce corn, the plant must have a strong, well-developed root system. In a matter of a few weeks, the corn stem breaks through the surface of the soil and continues the natural process of developing a stalk, leaves, and in due season mature ears of corn.

There are important lessons to learn from the corn seed that relates to you. You have been encoded with special talents, abilities, desires, and passions for life. They are inside you waiting to be placed in an environment that is conducive to growth. There are things to imagine that you haven't imagined. There are things to achieve that you haven't achieved yet. All of these unlimited possibilities are in you waiting to be stimulated to come forth.

Recognize that there is a natural process to maximizing your potential. Igniting the power of your potential begins as an internal process and more specifically a mental and spiritual process. In due time the real "you" will become obvious to others. Here is a word of caution. Don't expect everyone to be happy about your transformation. There will be people who will try to hinder your growth by reminding you of who you used to be.

The fact that a corn seed starts out very small has absolutely no bearing on its ability to develop a stalk seven feet tall with eighteen inch leaves and delicious ears of corn. Don't despise the day of small beginnings. Your past is not as important as your future. Don't let others minimize your potential. The purpose of this book is to create an environment in your mind that will cause all of the potential within you to expand past the barriers that have limited your rise to the surface. **It is time to experience the fullness of everything that has been encoded in you.**

The Birth of a Dream

After addressing a national convention of business executives, an older lady came over to me and said that she had been coming to national conventions for years, and for the first time, she felt like she had to act on what the speaker said.

She went on to explain that for years, she wanted to write a children's book and use her artistic abilities to illustrate the story. She said that for years she had been putting it off and allowing the hectic pace of her job and other responsibilities to get in the way of fulfilling her dream. She held my hand and tears began to well up in her eyes, she said, "When I get back to my hotel room I'm going to start on my book today."

As I stood there, I watched a metamorphosis take place right before my eyes. I saw that dear lady break out of the confines of her seed. She placed herself in an environment that was conducive to the growth of her dream. I cannot stress how important it is to be in an environment that is supportive, and encouraging. I will discuss the importance of your environment further in a later chapter.

By the time I had finished speaking, she had become so empowered by my words, the possibility of the book could no longer lie in a dormant state. That lady left that convention a changed person. I believe it's just a matter of time before her book will become a reality. That lady was past the point of just having a fleeting emotional experience. I have files filled with letters from the old and young alike who have been inspired to release the power of their potential.

From Dream Building to Homebuilding

I totally understood what was happening to that lady and the countless others like her who hear me speak. I also had a life-changing experience that caused one of my dreams to become reality.

It happened a number of years ago when I was working as a construction manager for a small homebuilding company in Houston, Texas. I thoroughly enjoyed my job. I was responsible for overseeing the construction of homes from start to finish.

While I was working for the company, I realized that the small company was not expanding and the possibility of me getting a promotion was slim. I was experienced in every aspect of the home building process from design to construction, from marketing to financing. I began to think about starting my own homebuilding company.

At that point all I had was a wealth of knowledge and experience, but I had no capital to start a first-class homebuilding company. The idea of starting a company began to weigh heavily on my mind. Soon the thought of starting my own company began to be an obsession.

I began to think and conduct myself like a senior executive of a homebuilding company. I began to dress differently. Instead of coming to work in denim jeans and a pull-over shirt, I started wearing starched pants and shirts with buttons and a collar. My change in attitude and appearance did not go unnoticed. The guys in the field were never at a loss for negative comments.

However, their comments did not cause me to change or abandon my dream. I started collecting the business cards of subcontractors and suppliers. I started reading homebuilding magazines and books on how to start a business. I attended workshops and seminars on marketing and advertising. I started collecting marketing packages from every builder in the Houston area.

Every weekend I would visit different homebuilders in residential communities. I would spend hours walking through their model homes. I studied every element of the homes from the foundation to the roof. I made notes on effective interior decorating and landscaping ideas. I studied their marketing brochures and became familiar with the floor plans from over 20 different builders.

I began to inquire about how much capital was needed to start the company. I was told by a number of bankers who worked with builders that I would need about three to four million dollars for operating capital and construction lines of credit. At that time, my wife was pregnant with our second daughter and I barely had three to four hundred dollars to spare. I did not have a clue where I was going to get millions of dollars.

One bank president was so intrigued by my confidence that I could pull it all together that he took time to drive me around Houston to show me where to find the best subdivisions to begin building homes. Even though I did not have everything I needed, whenever I spoke to individuals about the prospects of my company I conveyed a strong sense of confidence. I let them know that whatever it would take to get it done, I would do it. I knew that if I did not have confidence in myself no one else would either. I could not afford to let doubt and fear keep me from my goal.

A Million Dollar Message

Everything changed when I heard a message by Dr. Miles Munroe. Dr. Munroe is an international teacher and speaker from Nassau, Bahamas. He spoke on "Giving Birth to Your Dreams." As I sat there in the audience, I absorbed every word he said.

During the course of the message, my dream of starting a homebuilding company broke free from all the limitations I had encountered. I began to feel a tear welling up in my eye. I tried my best to clear it away before it became too obvious, but while I was dealing with the first tear, another began to well up in my other eye. Before I knew it, tears were streaming out of both eyes faster than I could wipe them away. I was experiencing a transformation.

In that meeting, my homebuilding company became real to me. Every doubt and concern that had hindered me from making plans for my company was dissolved in the tears flowing down my face. I knew without a doubt, that I would have my company. The money, and the assistance I needed would come. All I had to do was begin to take the first steps and every thing I needed would arrive exactly when I needed it. I left that meeting a changed man.

To conclude the story, within a year of attending that meeting, I had found a business partner and developed a business plan. We attracted investment capital, and we secured residential lots for the homes in an attractive subdivision. We obtained construction financing and the company was a reality. If I had not placed myself in an environment that was conducive to productivity, I would never have heard Dr. Miles Munroe. I might have missed my appointment with destiny.

You owe it to yourself to place yourself in an environment that is favorable to growth and productivity. The seeds of success that are encoded in you will lead you to your destiny. Many times the desires of your heart are an indication of what has been encoded in you. Avoid the temptation to place limits on your possibilities.

Don't get discouraged by the way circumstances and situations may appear on the surface. You must develop faith and confidence for a brighter future and a better life. The Bible states that without faith it is impossible to please God. Psalm 37 reveals that if you find pleasure in pleasing God, He will give you the desires of your heart. If you meet the conditions, you can receive the promise. Many times God plants desires in our hearts and then directs us down a path so He can fulfill them.

What have you put off doing? What have you convinced yourself you could never achieve? No excuse is worth delaying your success. Your seed is already encoded for your success. How long will you delay your rise to the surface?

It's time to pause and take action. When we are children, the world seems full of unlimited possibilities. We feel we can be anything and achieve anything we want without limitations. However, as we grow older the youthful optimism begins to dissipate. The realities of the cruel negative world begin to exert their influence on our hopes and dreams.

It's time to return to the days of youthful optimism. Imagine that there are no limitations on what you can achieve, where you can go, what you can learn, and what income you can earn. In a limitless environment, how would you change your life?

Taking Action to Succeed

Write things that you would like to achieve or experience. Write down the areas in which you want to focus the reconditioning of your mind for success. Write down the kind of income you would like to earn and how you want to enhance your career. What can you do to improve or end unproductive relationships? What would you like to do in your leisure time. Where would you like to visit? Make sure you take the time to write these things down, we will revisit them in a later chapter. Complete this exercise *before* moving on to the next lesson.

These are the things I would like to achieve or experience.

In my thoughts ____

____

____

In my finances ____

____

____

In my career ____

____

____

In my personal relationships ______________________________

____

____

"You must believe in yourself, my son,
or no one else will believe in you.
Be self-confident, self-reliant,
and even if you don't make it,
you will know you have done your best.
Now, go to it."

Mary Hardy MacArthur
Wife of General Douglas MacArthur

I am an original, I am one-of-a-kind and highly valued by God who has endowed me with special abilities and talents to fulfill my divine assignment.

Lesson Four

Strengthen Your Self-Esteem

The feeling of significance is vitally important to your mental, emotional, spiritual and social well-being. The natural need to feel that we are important is a driving force within us all. To think bigger, maximize your potential, and achieve your dreams and goals, you must have a strong sense of who you are and what you can accomplish.

Those who experience success and personal fulfillment must practice self-esteem strengthening activities to insure continued success. It is similar to body building. If you don't take deliberate action to combat the negative effects of our society, eventually it will take its toll on you.

On a regular basis I have to manage negative comments, innuendoes and circumstances that are designed to challenge my self-esteem, but because I know who I am and why I am here, what others say will never deter me from achieving my goals.

I recognize them as attacks on my accomplishments and attacks on my mental and spiritual well-being. I don't allow the limiting beliefs of others to hinder me from thinking bigger. I stand on God's promise that no evil device designed to hinder me will be effective. The principles I am sharing with you helps me to remain focused as I charge full speed ahead.

No Discounting Allowed

Self-defeating beliefs are very common in people who have self-images that are out of alignment with their natural talents and abilities. I have discovered that everyone has positive attributes. In my presentations, I often ask my audience to list their positive attributes. For some this is an easy assignment. However, for others it presents a considerable challenge. Some people really don't believe they have anything of value residing in them.

Sometimes it is easier to see positive attributes in others than to recognize the gifts of greatness within yourself. **Don't diminish the value of your own skills or abilities and don't inflate the value of the skills or abilities of others.**

When you begin to compare yourself with others based on success or failures, professional status and finances, be careful not to overestimate their achievements in life and underestimate your own success. If you stop and really consider your life and all you have been through, I'm positive you have success stories to tell. **Don't discount who you are, what you have, or what you have accomplished.**

By valuing yourself, you allow others to value you too. You must work diligently to eliminate the mental barriers that limit your own growth and your ability to think bigger. Give yourself permission to move past what has happened in the past. **Your yesterdays are not as important as your tomorrows.** You can determine your own circumstances; they don't have to determine you. If your present circumstances are not favorable for achieving success and dynamic living, then its time to change them.

Set Up to Fail

Regrettably, I must admit that I find low self-esteem quite common among a considerable portion of our youth. We live in an age of rapid change. Many of our kids are trying to determine how and where they fit in their families, in their schools, and in society. Unfortunately for some kids, their dreams, ability, appearance and intelligence have been marginalized by peers, parents, and teachers. The end result is that they begin to believe what they repeatedly hear about themselves, even if what is being said is not true.

Once you accept false debilitating statements as truth, they breed feelings of inferiority. When you feel you are inferior, you will resign yourself to live a low-level life. The feelings of inferiority then mutates into feelings of selfishness, hopelessness, and anger. If these feelings of inferiority are developed during childhood, the child is at risk of spending the rest of his life in a mediocre state of existence. As an adult, he carries these feelings of inferiority with him. The downward cycle will continue unless he is taught how to end the cycle of low-level thinking and begin to think bigger.

Inferiority creates a feeling of unworthiness. Studies of high achievers confirm that positive self-esteem is essential for success. Managers and salespersons who doubt their own self-worth often experience momentary success. They top-out very quickly and then began to regress or lose their drive to progress. The top achievers possess positive attitudes and feelings about themselves because they understand that the true gage of success is not predicated on external circumstances as much as it is with a core belief of their own potential, ability and individual self-worth.

I have the privilege of speaking to people from all walks of life, including those who are down and out as well as those who seem to have it all. Low self-esteem is not a respecter of persons. There are plenty of high level senior executives who feel as though they are carrying the weight of the entire company and their stockholders on their shoulders. The challenges of daily operations combined with global competition, threat of mergers and downsizing can slowly erode their confidence in their ability to hold it all together. For many executives and managers, positive self-esteem is connected to their ability to control their business environment. Remember you are not defined by your title, or your job. You are defined by your view of your self-worth, abilities, and commitment to maximize your potential.

Don't Believe the Hype

It is very easy to succumb to the constant flow of negative messages that we receive constantly on a deliberate and subliminal basis. Billions of dollars are spent each year by advertisers to make us feel that unless we buy their product, we are missing out on life. These messages are directed at us not to build us up, but to make us weak. Commercials are repeated on a daily basis because advertisers realize if we hear a message long enough, we will begin to believe what we hear.

The commercial advertisers recognize that we all have an internal need to be loved, to be wanted, to be important, to be treated with dignity and respect. Because of the generally negative world we live in, far too many people feel those internal desires will never materialize for them.

Many individuals try to mask their low self-esteem with condescending attitudes, aggressive behavior or the illusions of prosperity and status. They unconsciously begin calling more attention to themselves because of their low self-esteem. Those who are truly comfortable with who they are and what they have don't have to flaunt their success to prove they are successful.

Low self-esteem, anger, and guilt are barriers to thinking bigger and achieving more. Your self-image is a product of your environment. Your environment is comprised of what you see, hear, and feel on a continuous basis. Develop your own commercial messages and replay them continually in your mind. Remind yourself that you have a special purpose and a specific assignment. Later in this book I will share specific methods for developing your own self-esteem strengthening commercials.

You can begin the process of strengthening your self–esteem by reading aloud the affirmations at the beginning of each chapter. Read them aloud daily. And put them to work in your life. If you daily think self-esteem strengthening thoughts, you will begin to believe the positive things you state about yourself. You will then begin to act on what you believe. **You can determine your own circumstances. They don't have to determine you.**

Move Your "But" Out of the Way

Many times we are our own worst enemy when it comes to being a bigger thinker and maximizing our potential. How many times have you had a thought about doing something new or different and in a split second your self-defeating beliefs told you why it would not or could not work? Take the limits off of your ability to think bigger and succeed. **The only limits you face are the limits you set in place.** In my seminars I often hear people say, "I could be like that," or " I wish I could do that," and in the second breath they immediately develop a reason why it will never happen for them. "I would, *but* I can't. Behind every "*but*" is a reason not to think bigger and maximize their potential.

"I would like to get a promotion, *but* I would have to get a masters degree and learn how to use a computer."

"I would like to start my own business, *but* I just don't have the time and I'm too old."

"I really would like to try out for the cheerleading squad, *but* I could never be good enough to get selected."

"I think I could represent our district well as a city council member, *but* I'm not good at campaigning or raising money.

Those who are successful use constructive self-talk daily. You can talk yourself into success just as easily as you can talk yourself into failure. Always keep your self-talk positive.

Dora Who?

When I was appointed to the Fort Bend County Housing Finance Corporation, I had the privilege of serving with Mrs. Dora Olivo. Dora is a lawyer and always has had a deep commitment to advancing the community.

One day at our board meeting, she announced that she was going to run for State Representative for the 27th District in Texas. She had no formal political experience. She did not have a lot of money, she did not have name recognition, her husband was not a wealthy businessman, and she had a son in college to support. Dora did not have most of the things the political experts indicate you need to win a campaign. What she did have was a genuine unrelenting passion to make a difference in the lives of people in her district.

She began a small, grass-roots campaign and called on everyone she knew to lend their money and their energy to her efforts. It was hard to say "No" to Dora because she is a hard working, mild mannered, unassuming person with deep moral and spiritual values.

She even pulled me into the process. Before I knew it, I was putting out yard signs and making phone calls encouraging residents to vote for her. Dora Olivo won the election and continues to be reelected to represent the district. She could have come up with numerous legitimate reasons why she could not run for office. I am glad she did not let obstacles stop her from fulfilling her dream.

Never let your "*but*" get in the way of following your dreams. Self-defeating beliefs don't give up their territory easily. Some of your hindering beliefs are deeply rooted in your mind, and they must be uprooted, cast out of your mind and never allowed to return. Conditioning yourself to think bigger and achieve more is serious business. Don't take it lightly. The quality of your life will be determined by how committed you are to changing your life.

25 exercises for strengthening your self-esteem

1. Experience success daily by accomplishing daily goals.

2. Focus on your strengths while improving your weaknesses.

3. Find at least one thing to be happy about.

4. Give someone a compliment.

5. Practice walking with confidence, shoulders back, head, and eyes lifted.

6. Introduce yourself to someone you don't know.

7. Read a book about someone you admire or someone who has overcome obstacles.

8. Anytime you interact with a person with a name tag on, call them by their name.

9. Don't go to sleep watching the late night news.

10. Use positive, bold and descriptive words to describe how you are doing. (Great, Incredibly Blessed, Super Fantastic)

11. Smile more.

12. Take action to overcome fears.

13. Sing happy songs in the shower.

14. Learn something new every day.

15. Spend time in prayer.

16. Offer to help someone.

17. Sit on the front row.

18. Ask a question in a class or meeting.

19. Confidently greet people as you pass them.

20. Remind yourself that your attitude determines your altitude.

21. Practice making eye contact.

22. Practice thinking like a winner.

23. Identify ways to improve your performance at home, school or work, then do it.

24. Avoid negative people and negative conversations.

25. Don't procrastinate, just do it.

It's time to pause and take action. We all have experiences and emotions that serve as the source of many self-defeating thoughts. Those who are successful learn to develop a mental defense system for self-defeating attitudes, emotions and thoughts. You have to take personal responsibility for building and protecting your self-esteem and realizing your dreams.

Taking Action to Succeed

List four areas in your life that need improving. List four ways you can improve those areas in your life. Commit yourself to making changes in your life. Sign and date this page. Those who are successful resist procrastinating. I really do expect you to follow through with this exercise and only move to the next lesson when the exercise is completed !!

Four things I do well are:

1.____

____

____

2.____

____

____

3.____

____

____

4.____

____

____

Four areas in my life that need improvement are:

1.____

____

2.____

____

3.____

____

4.____

____

Four ways I can improve specific areas in my life are:

1.____

____

2.____

____

3.____

____

4.____

____

Signature   Date

____

**"I had heard all kinds of rumors about MIT.
They used to say
that even the janitors at MIT
had master's degrees.
At first I was not going
but then I could not run away from a
challenge.
I had to compete with the best."**

Ronald McNair
Challenger Astronaut

I will always remember that on the other side of the mountains of my fears and failures is the green valley of my success.

Lesson Five

Conquer Your Fears

Fear is the archenemy of success. The thing you fear most will become reality. You can't learn more by concentrating on how hard it is for you to learn new information. You can't close a sale if you concentrate on how many sales you have not closed. You cannot lose weight concentrating on how overweight you are.

When you fear something be aware that you are creating a subconscious directive to achieve the very thing you fear. Unconsciously the thing you fear gets translated into your desired objective. That is why it is so important to concentrate on succeeding instead of concentrating on failing. Focus on the positive and resist the temptation to focus on the negative.

Fear paralyzes people and keeps them from seizing opportunities. Fear keeps us from speaking up and stepping out. In addition, fear has negative physical effects ranging from constant fatigue to premature death. In this lesson we will take time to identify some common fears and provide practical instructions on how to overcome them.

President Franklin D. Roosevelt, on the eve of the United States entering World War II, advised the American people that the only thing we had to fear was fear itself. **Fear will snatch success from your hands in a split second.**

I am reminded of the Bible story of the twelve spies who were sent out to explore the "Promised Land" for Moses. The spies came back with incredible accounts of the fertility and wealth of the land. However, they also reported that there were extremely large people, "giants," that inhabited the land.

Joshua and Caleb were the only two spies out of twelve who wanted to go and take control of the land which God had already given to them. The people decided not to move forward because of the giants in the land. Because of fear, an entire nation of approximately three million people wandered in the wilderness for forty years at the entrance to their land of promise.

Fear is the reason why millions achieve less and settle for less. They see giants and become afraid. Giants always take up residence in the Promised Land. Those who are successful at possessing the land must conquer the giants. Make a decision this very minute that you will not allow fear to keep you from entering your "Promised Land," or fulfilling your destiny, or achieving your dreams, and desires. How much time have you wasted wandering in the wilderness of unfulfilled potential?

Cultivating the Seeds of Success

I have had a multitude of challenges in my life. The first major battle with the fear of failure occurred when I was an architecture student at Prairie View A& M University (PVAMU). The summer I started college, it became very clear that I was not academically prepared for college. I was sorely deficient in math and science but I was determined to do what was necessary to excel.

I started attending every study session that was offered. Although I knew it would be a challenge, I was determined to master the courses. I would draw in the architecture lab until midnight, go to bed and wake up at three o'clock and study until six o'clock in the morning. Surprisingly, I found that when I studied after I had gotten some rest and when I had no distractions, I would have almost perfect recall of the information. It was like putting the information on a computer disk in my brain. Whenever I needed the information it was easy to retrieve it from my mental file.

During the fall semesters, I made a conscious effort to form friendships with students who were excelling, and joined their study groups. I continued my early morning study routine and my grades improved significantly. The last semester of my freshman year I earned a 4.0 grade point average with 21 course credits. I would never recommend anyone take 21 hours of courses in one semester. However, no one told me it could not be done, so I did it.

I applied the principles in this book to my own academic challenges and I experienced incredible results. During my course of study I achieved considerable academic success. I was on the Dean's List and honor roll for six consecutive semesters. I had been transformed from an underachiever to a superachiever in less than a year.

During my fourth year in college, my instructor and counselor, Simon Wiltz, began to challenge me to consider graduate school. I had often discussed with him my desire to become a real estate developer. My goal was to graduate and begin working at a real estate development company. I wanted to know everything about designing, constructing, financing buildings and owning buildings.

One day he told me there was a computer-aided drafting conference in Boston, Massachusetts, and he wanted to take me and several other students to the conference. After arriving in Boston, we found out his primary reason for going to the conference was to give us the grand tour of his alma mater the Massachusetts Institute of Technology (MIT) and introduce us to his friends in Boston and at Harvard.

All Simon Wiltz talked about during the entire trip was graduate school. He felt that it was his personal obligation to expose us to every opportunity available to us, and he did so with an unrelenting passion. I have tremendous admiration for the many instructors and administrators at PVAMU who are committed to helping students maximize their potential.

MIT or Bust

After we returned from our trip to Boston, I began to seriously consider applying to MIT. The Center for Real Estate Development had just been established, and there was not another school in the country where I could learn the business of real estate development. I learned that I could get a Master's Degree in City Planning and specialize in real estate development. I began to put my application package together, and the word began to spread on our small university campus. My instructors had so much confidence in me that they started spreading the word that I was *going* to MIT. I had not completed and submitted the application package, and the word was spreading that I was *going* to MIT.

It Hit Me Like a Cement Truck

That is when the fear of failure hit me like a cement truck. Approximately sixty students would be accepted into the Master of City Planning program. They received hundreds of applications from all over the world. How could I be sure that they would accept mine? Even more pressure was added when I was told that I would be the first graduate of PVAMU ever to attend MIT. I felt like I was carrying the hopes and aspirations of an entire university on my shoulders, and my knees were beginning to get weak.

"What" questions bombarded my mind. "What if I failed to get accepted? What would my friends say? What would my instructors say?" I had never failed at any major project. Now my educational advancement was in the hands of strangers on the application review committee. The fear of failure began to consume me, and shortly after I submitted my application, I felt like calling MIT and asking them to remove mine from the pile.

Streams In The Desert

Then one day something clicked in my mind and spirit. I came to my senses. Instead of spending valuable time contemplating failure, I started developing a strategy for success. While I never completely got over the butterflies in my stomach, I did not let the fear of failure stop me from focusing on success. I decided I would work as though everything depended on me and pray as though everything depended on God. My prayer life dramatically increased, and so did my peace of mind.

Whenever I would feel anxiety building, I would remind God that He said that those who trust Him would be the head and not the tail. I would be above and not beneath. I reminded Him that He promised that if I walked according to His word that whatever I did would prosper. The most comforting scripture of all was *2 Timothy 1:7 God has not given us a spirit of fear but of love, power, and a sound mind.*

The deadline for receiving acceptance notices from MIT passed, and I had not received a letter from the admissions committee. During that time I was an intern at the Houston Metropolitan Transit Authority. My boss and dear friend Lenwood Howell would ask me every day if I had heard from MIT. After weeks went by with no response, Lenwood insisted that I call. Words can't express the tidal wave of fear that gripped me as I placed the call to the admissions office.

To my utter amazement I was told that I had been accepted, and that a letter had been sent to me weeks before. At that moment I think I felt every emotion known to man, simultaneously. I walked into Lenwood's office in a state of paralyzing shock.

Immediately my mind was assaulted by negative thoughts. I began to ask myself, "What in the world had I done?" Now I would have to move to a cold, expensive city where I didn't know anyone. I had voluntarily committed myself to a rigorous and demanding course of study at one of the most prestigious universities in the world. Had I lost my mind? I must have been insane to submit that application. How was I going to handle all the pressure? After five years of studying at PVAMU, I was already mentally exhausted. It would be so much easier to just go and get a good paying job!

Blazing The Trail

Despite all my initial reservations, I did well at MIT and graduated two years later with a Master's Degree in City Planning, specializing in housing and real estate development. The following year my PVAMU classmate Verna René Hunter was accepted into the program, and the next year another PVAMU classmate of ours, Regina Blair was accepted.

Today I hate to think how I could have missed my appointment with destiny if I had allowed my fear of failure to derail my application to graduate school. I had no idea that my admission would open the door for my fellow classmates and other students at PVAMU.

From Fearful to Fearless

The best way to overcome fear is to meet it head-on with confidence. All confidence is developed. No one is born with confidence. The successful develop confidence by taking action on a consistent basis. **Taking action minimizes fear.** Indecision and procrastination only strengthen fear. Go ahead and do whatever is causing your fear. You'll find that what you feared wasn't as bad as you thought. Whenever fear comes knocking on your door, send your confidence and faith to answer it, and fear will flee.

Most of our fears are caused by experiences and events in our past or by what we've been told by others. Successful people identify their fears, find the source of their fears and master the things that stand in the way of their success.

The next time you find yourself becoming anxious or fearful, instead of saying "I'm afraid," say "I'm excited!" They both provide adrenaline impulses, but one leaves you fearful and the other leaves you fearless.

For many people fear is like an unhealthy addiction. It hurts them to let go even if it is negatively impacting them. If it hurts you to let go of your fears, then maybe you are addicted. Your fear may have become like a close friend. People who are addicted to fear will always be hindered from maximizing their potential. Let's take a quick look at some common fears so we can put them to rest, forever.

These five common fears evolve into a paralyzing state of not being able to make good decisions. To be successful you must overcome the fear of:

1. **Poverty** – overcome the fear of poverty by maximizing your present financial resources as you diligently explore avenues for wealth without worry.

2. **Criticism** – don't worry about what other people think, do or say. Accept constructive suggestions as you peruse your dreams with a passion. Remember when you decide to crawl out of the pit of mediocrity, someone will always try to pull you back.

3. **Failure** – Every successful person has experienced failure; it is a natural part of the success process. Learn everything you can from every failure, and keep moving forward.

4. **Worry** – Decide here and now to liberate yourself from all forms of worry. Worry has never changed any situation and never will. It is the most unproductive use of mental capacity known to man. Use your mental abilities to change the things you can change, commit the rest to God's hands and then sleep peacefully.

5. **Success** – For some this is the greatest fear of all. If you succeed once, then you will know what it takes to succeed again. Consistently set goals that are attainable, enjoy the fruit of your labor and enhance the lives of others.

Don't Take Failure Personally

Another aspect of transforming yourself is learning how to handle failure effectively. For a long time I thought that successful people never had failures or disappointments. Successful people always seemed to be happy and enjoying life without a care. As I grew older, I realized I was terribly mistaken. Every person who has achieved anything in life has experienced failure. Most of the time the media focuses on their success rather than examining how many times they failed *before* they became successful.

Failure is present along every path to success. The difference between those who succeed and those who don't is that **the successful use failure as a stepping stone not a stumbling stone.** Failure is attracted to those who allow themselves to be failure conscious instead of success conscious. Don't allow yourself to be consumed with the thought of failing. Use your mental and physical abilities to concentrate on succeeding.

Dennis is Not a Menace

My friend Dennis taught me many years ago how important it is not to throw in the towel. Dennis was Chairman of the Board of an organization where I served as the Executive Director. I learned that several years before I joined the organization, Dennis had owned a bank and was a very successful real estate developer. He was a multi-millionaire before the age of thirty.

When the Houston economy took a nose dive, crashed, and burned, Dennis lost everything he had worked so hard to achieve. Many of the people he thought were friends gave him the cold shoulder. Although he and his family endured tremendous financial hardships, he always had a positive attitude. Nothing could stop him from being hopeful about his future. He started a bottled water company; eventually it failed. He started a notebook computer company, that failed also. He got a job as a money manager for a well capitalized investor and things began to stabilize.

During a lunch meeting, a business associate asked me why was I spending so much time getting to know Dennis Murphree. "Don't you know he's failed at all of those businesses" he commented. I told him that Dennis was the only person that I had a personal relationship with who was a millionaire before he was thirty. I was confident that if he made a million and lost it, eventually he could make another million and keep it.

I knew it was just a matter of time before Dennis would rebound. I needed to learn as much from Dennis as I could, while I had the opportunity. It's not often you can draw from the wisdom and experience of a person of his caliber.

Several years later, I called on Dennis when I needed help raising capital for my homebuilding company and he assembled a group of investors for the company. Today Murphree Venture Partners is a nationally recognized investment capital firm headquartered in Houston with offices in four states. His determination has paid off and he is reaping the rewards of not giving up. Dennis is a living example of how diligence can pay off when you don't give up.

Don't accept defeat as being anything more than a temporary setback. Experiencing setbacks in life does not mean you are a failure. A failure is a person who has blundered, but is not able to profit from the experience. Remember your past failures just long enough to learn from them and move on.

One of the most common causes of failure is the tendency to throw in the towel when faced with challenges. Every failure carries with it the seed of an equal success. **To achieve success you must stay focused and turn your defeats into victories.**

Those who are successful recognize that failure is an enemy of success. It often tries to discourage you when success is right at your fingertips. Remember the old saying, "Quitters never win and winners never quit." If you are a quitter, you will not experience success.

We all will encounter disappointments and failures on the road to success. Successful people experience numerous heartbreaking and soul wrenching challenges before they arrive at their destination. **The key to success is to stand boldly in the middle of your challenges and believe for success without wavering.** You must replace your fear of failure with a desire to succeed.

Successful people weather the storms of life by bending and not breaking. If your *push* to succeed is strong enough, then the *pull* to fail will never keep you from your goal. **Persistence is the most effective tool for maneuvering through resistance.** Decide to become immune to fear and blind to the possibility of failure. For the successful, failure is not an option.

It's time to pause and take action. Those who are successful in life must overcome fears and take action to achieve their goals. Think about your dreams and goals. What are the fears that are hindering you from moving forward?

Taking Action to Succeed

Consider the lessons you have learned from some of your failures. What would you do differently to get a better result? Then proceed to list your goals and desires. Under each one write a common fear that restricts you from taking action. On the third line identify the action you *will* take to get past your fears so your can move forward.

1.____

____

____

2.____

____

____

3.____

____

____

4.____

____

____

"What a man believes in his mind, he achieves
What a man believes in his mind, he receives
What a man believes in his mind,
controls his actions
What a man believes in his mind,
directs his passions
What a man believes in his mind,
becomes the rails that guide the train,
on which he is the conductor."

T.R. Williams
Speaker/Author

I will restrict my mind to a diet of bountiful beliefs rich in positive possibilities, opulent opportunities and remarkable realities.

Lesson Six

Expel Beliefs that Limit Potential

When I was young, much of the excitement surrounding Christmas was anticipating what gifts Santa Clause would bring. I believed that a robust bearded man dressed in a red and white suit would sneak into our home and leave gifts under our Christmas tree. I believed it because that is what I was told by those I respected.

This myth was reinforced by the presence of Santa's helpers in all of the malls and television programs. For a while I was convinced that Santa was real and I acted according to my beliefs. When I grew older I realized that what I had been taught to believe was not true. I then changed how I responded to men dressed in red Santa suites. I stopped putting out milk and cookies on Christmas Eve. I changed my behavior to correspond with my change in belief.

A belief is a firmly entrenched view of things by which all additional information is validated. Beliefs are filters for our perception of everything around us. What you have been conditioned to believe about yourself will dominate your life.

When you believe something is true, then you automatically begin to act as if it's true. If you believe something is impossible for you to achieve, then your mind will prevent you from being able to achieve it. You are only limited by your ability to believe what is possible for you.

Every successful person at some point goes through the process of analyzing the beliefs that hold him back and those that propel him forward. The deeply held beliefs you have will dictate how you view yourself, your quality of life, and regulate your level of success and fulfillment. **Your beliefs can light the path to success and empower you to travel to your destination. They can also render you powerless and disorientated in the darkness of mediocrity and failure.**

Your present beliefs are the result of your social environment, past personal experiences and information received from others as truth. When you know how beliefs are established, you can create new beliefs that are in line with your new desires for achievement and fulfillment.

However, before you can begin the process of creating new beliefs, you must first identify beliefs that are presently limiting your actions and thoughts. Then you must establish your present hindering beliefs as false and undesirable.

For some, this can be a challenge because if done properly, it will require facing serious issues and require you to unload unnecessary baggage you have been carrying around. The process of self-examination can be painful. However, it will be revealing and allow you to break free from the chains of your past.

It's time to pause and take action. In my workshops, I ask the audience to take time to write down the beliefs or circumstances that they feel are presently obstacles to their success. This is a good place for you to stop and think about beliefs you carry that are hindering your advancement.

Taking Action to Succeed

List four key beliefs or circumstances that have limited your success. Take your time and examine your beliefs. Hold them up to the light of truth so you can see them with crystal clarity. You may need to dig deep into the recesses of your mind to excavate beliefs that have been hindering you all of your life.

Once you have listed four hindering beliefs, under each one list an empowering belief or a change in circumstance that will support your goals and desires for success and personal fulfillment.

1.____

2.____

3.____

4.____

Let's address 4 common hindering beliefs.

1. The first common hindering belief **- I don't deserve something better.** You deserve whatever you think you should have. Life is like a buffet dinner. There is plenty to put on your plate. An assorted array of delicious delicacies are yours for the taking. If the only thing you choose to select is a glass of water and crackers, don't blame the others who are eating heartily and going back for seconds.

If this is your first time being invited to the "buffet dinner of life" and you feel a little unsure of how it all works, watch what others are doing and do likewise. If you want to be successful, do what successful people do, go where successful people go, and talk like successful people talk. Don't be reluctant or shy. The successful seize every opportunity to get the most out of life. Practice walking with confidence, talking with confidence and thinking with confidence. Fight the temptation to talk yourself out of what can be yours if you really want it.

For some of you, believing that you deserve better and that you can have what you want out of life is a far-fetched concept. Take an honest look at your present circumstances and your living and working environment. **On a daily basis tell yourself that you can do better and you deserve better.** To do this doesn't cost you any money. You can be broke, busted, or disgusted and still do this. In fact, if you are broke, busted, or disgusted you can't afford *not* to do it. **I have found that those who really want change will do whatever it takes. Those who don't will continue to repeat the same mistakes.** As sure as you are holding this book in your hands, things can change for you.

By *speaking* to your circumstances and environment, you will be creating a new belief. Every time you identify something that is not what you want in your life, tell it to go because it doesn't belong in your life anymore. You will find that your comfort zone will begin to change. Things that you used to accept you will no longer be comfortable accepting. As you reinforce your new belief system, your mind will begin to remind you that you are uncomfortable in your present situation and you must do something to change it.

Expanding my comfort zone took some time and great effort. After I read the book *Think and Grow Rich* by Napoleon Hill, I was determined to see the professional and financial aspects of my life advance to a higher level. Mr. Hill told me exactly what to do.

In his revealing book, *Mental Toughness for Success,* Dr. I.V. Hilliard presented a step-by-step process for reconditioning my mind for success. Other than the Bible, *Think and Grow Rich* and *Mental Toughness for Success* have been the two greatest tools in assisting me in my transformation. After reading these books, I began to tell myself I deserved better, and I would not settle for second best.

I'll Be Paying In Cash

I remember when I decided that I deserved to drive a Mercedes-Benz. At the time my wife and I had one car which is almost unheard of in Houston. She would carpool to work, and I drove our emerald green four-door 740 Volvo. I didn't know much about Mercedes-Benz cars, so I started visiting the dealership and asking questions about their cars.

I began to visit the dealership on a monthly basis. I would go and sit in the lobby just to get comfortable in the surroundings. One of the salesmen would let me go out and sit in the car. I imagined myself driving the car with the sunroof opened and feeling the sun on my face.

One day the salesman asked me if I would like to complete a credit application for a vehicle. I told him that would not be necessary because I would be paying cash for my car. At that moment, I didn't have any money to pay cash for the car. However that did not stop me from looking or asking questions.

I straightened up my garage to make room for my Mercedes-Benz. I began to tell my children that we were going to get a new car. Every time we would get in the Volvo, we would talk about our Mercedes-Benz. I was deliberately expanding my comfort zone and creating a belief that I deserved better. My mind began to direct my actions to bring it to pass.

I've had people in my seminars say, "That sounds like foolishness. You can't just talk your way into a new future." Believe me; this is not foolishness. However, it does require faith. You must believe that what you are saying will really happen for you. If you don't believe you deserve better, you'll never have anything better.

A year later I paid cash for my Mercedes-Benz and drove it off the lot. The point is that change did not occur until I decided that I deserved it. You may not need a car. You may want to move from vice president to president of the division or company, or improve your grades. Maybe you want to buy a home or increase your income.

Don't convince yourself to settle for second best. Stand for the specific things that you want out of life and work to obtain them. Never limit your possibilities. This principle will work for you if you work the principle.

DON'T YOU THINK IT'S TIME YOU
DESERVED SOMETHING BETTER?

***2. The second common hindering belief.* I must be accepted by others to feel good about myself –** The only one you need acceptance from is God. If you please Him, everything else will eventually work out. You cannot be successful trying to please everybody. When people realize that you are easily manipulated, they will take advantage of you and kick you to the curb when you are of no further use to them.

You are an original; one of a kind. You are the last of your kind, and you are priceless. You have a specific purpose, and everything you need to complete your assignment is already encoded in you. Your self-worth must radiate from the inside of you outward. If you are expecting your self-worth to flow from others into you, I guarantee you will always be disappointed.

During this period of your transformation, begin to focus your attention and efforts on addressing the issues of resentment, hostility and anger generally associated with this hindering belief. Numerous studies have found that many people who are manipulated often despise their manipulators and deeply resent the things they do to receive approval. Bitterness and resentment are barriers to success and purposeful living. Release the people and events of the past and move on.

How many times have you found yourself laughing at jokes that were not funny just so you could fit in? Have you ever agreed to do something just so you could be a part of the group? Early in my career I had to deal with issues of acceptance.

One day I came to the realization that I can't live my life like a chameleon lizard. I was changing colors to blend in to please every Tom, Dick and Harriet who supposedly had influence. I decided to be consistently consistent. Regardless of where I was and who I was with, I maintained the same character and moral standards. I didn't try to become everybody's friend. Surprisingly, I began to find myself meeting and networking with people who were of like mind and morals. **Remember: Birds of a feather flock together. It's time to leave the chickens alone and begin to soar with the eagles.**

***3. The third common hindering belief* - I have failed in the past, so I can never try again.** Your past does not have to dictate your future. Those who are successful never allow the failures of the past to stop their progress. If you have failed, you can't give up. There is life after a failed test, failed marriage, layoffs, and bankruptcy. Keep hanging in there until you succeed.

When a player on a basketball team takes a shot at the goal and misses, he doesn't quit the team in the middle of the game and take a seat in the stands. He hustles to get the ball again so he can try it again. No matter how many times he misses, his ultimate aim is to make points. It doesn't matter how many times you fail, stay in the game until you score. In the game of life some of your shots will be blocked, you will be fouled and be subject to bad calls from the referees. But don't quit while you still have time on the clock.

***4. The fourth common hindering belief* - I am the way I am and I can't change.** Change is the product of deliberate effort sustained over time. You can begin to change the moment you decide you sincerely want the benefits that change will bring. I am constantly amazed that some people will change jobs, spouses, and friends but never think about changing themselves.

The bigger thinkers are always in a state of change or growth. Successful people recognize that in most cases remaining the same is equivalent to stagnation. When you don't allow fresh ideas and new ways of doing things to impact your thinking, you will become a mentally stagnant person.

The truth of the matter is that people avoid making a commitment to change because it requires work. Some people are uninspired and want to take the easy route. Let me share a little secret with you. **Maintaining the status quo or taking the easy route never leads to long-term success and peak performance.** Decide today to change whatever needs changing, and begin the process now.

A New Name for a New Person

Faye was a smart and resourceful young wife with a young child. Her husband became involved with using and selling drugs. Tragically, Faye yielded to the temptation and became addicted to drugs. Her husband was arrested and sent to prison. She was left with a toddler and a newborn baby. Her drug habit so demoralized her that she lost all self-respect. Her family members tried to help her, but she continued on the downward spiral. The cumulative effect of drugs had sucked the life out of her spirit.

One day her mind cleared for a few hours. She began to think about her dreadful situation. She had come from a good home with loving parents. She had multiple talents and abilities, and yet she was throwing her life away to drugs. She decided that to remain the same would mean certain death. She had to do something that would set her free from the torment of drug dependency.

At that point the benefits associated with changing her situation far outweighed her need to remain the same. She was admitted to a rehabilitation center and she put her life back on track. She credits her recovery from the brink of death to God's mercy. Today she is happily married and living a fulfilling life. She has been drug free for many years. She no longer goes by the name Faye. She is now called by her first name, Vanessa. She says that the person known as Faye no longer exists. I'm proud to have Vanessa as my sister-in -law. **Change is possible in any situation when the benefits of changing outweigh the need to remain the same.**

If you are dealing with an addiction to alcohol, drugs, pornography, sex, food, or anything else, get help today. **Remember: To experience fulfillment, you must be free of any hindrances against maximizing your potential and discovering your destiny.** You may be able to temporarily hide you addiction but eventually it will become obvious.

Time to pause and take action. Take time to closely examine your life and your surroundings. What are the things you need to change? It's up to you to take personal responsibility for your advancement to a new level, peak performance, and dynamic living. No one can make the decision for you, and no one should be able to talk you out of your decision to change.

Taking Action to Succeed

List the things you would like to change in your life. Consider the following areas: relationships, finances, employment, personal attitude, your physical environment, personal health and spiritual development.

1.____

____

2.____

____

3.____

____

4.____

____

5.____

____

6.____

____

7.____

____

"To build my confidence I had to talk to myself. I would look in the mirror and say that what I have to impart is vitally important; people will pack auditoriums and convention halls to gain wisdom and insight from what I have to share. I'm not on an ego trip, but a divine mission to transform the lives of individuals and organizations."

T. R. Williams
Speaker/Author

Today is the first day of the rest of my life, I am stepping out, moving up and not giving in.
Look out world, here I come!

Lesson Seven

Develop a Confident Attitude

When my daughters were very young and beginning to learn how to sing, I focused on encouraging them to sing loudly and clearly. One day my wife walked in on one of our enthusiastic singing sessions and informed us that we were singing the wrong words and singing in the wrong key. I explained that we had plenty of time to teach the words and learn the correct key. I wasn't building musical ability, I was building confidence. Once kids are confident in their ability, they can learn anything. **Kids who believe they can accomplish anything will accomplish anything.** As adults we must avoid the temptation of limiting our kids based on our own perceived limitations.

Your belief will cause your mind to be creative, and you will find ways to accomplish much more than you ever dreamed. Believing you can succeed will cause others to have confidence in your ability. **A positive attitude is an outward sign of the confidence within**.

You can change your life just by changing your attitude. Your attitude is more important than your race, sex, height, or handicap. Your attitude is more important than your education, occupation, denomination, or political persuasion. Your attitude is more important than you age, ability, or aptitude. It will determine how high you will soar or whether you will just be sore.

Live in Great Expectation

The first novel I ever read was *Great Expectations* by Charles Dickens. Those who are bigger thinkers practice living with great expectations. An attitude of expectancy is like my American Express card, "I never leave home without it." It is required mental gear for the journey ahead. With a positive attitude, you will begin to attract positive people and positive things to you. Developing a confident attitude will draw others to you without you realizing it.

Those who experience the best that life has to offer expect the best. They expect achievement, professional advancement, higher incomes, improved relationships. They expect to make a difference in their family, workplace and community. You will become what you expect to become. Expect to excel and you will.

Early in my speaking career, I remember walking into a room of senior executives and managers. I was the keynote speaker at their professional businessmen's luncheon. As I stood at the podium, I noticed their long faces and blank stares. I did not know whether it reflected their doubt in my abilities, or maybe it was their lunch taking its toll.

Nevertheless, I fully expected to have their undivided attention. I expected to have them sitting at the edge of their chairs for the entire presentation. I believed that my enthusiasm and positive attitude were transmittable. I came at them with the force of an atomic bomb. Almost immediately they began to open up to my message. By the time the presentation was over, they were asking how soon could I come back. **Remember: Your attitude is a small thing that makes a huge difference**.

Something Good is Going to Happen

The international evangelist and educator, Dr. Oral Roberts, popularized the phrase *"Something good is going to happen to you this very day."* I had the pleasure of attending a meeting where Dr. Roberts was the speaker. During his message he asked all of those in attendance to stand and think about something that they desperately needed. I stood and remembered that my wife and I had decided to get completely out of debt.

I focused my thoughts and prayers on receiving additional money so we could pay off our debts. **Remember: Expectation creates an atmosphere of anticipation.** Later that afternoon, I returned home and we had received a letter from one of our creditors. The letter stated that our debt of $95,000 was cancelled. We no longer owed the company anything! Never underestimate the power of prayer when you expect something good to happen.

Avoid Sinking Thinking

It is what we do consistently that determines success or failure, victory or defeat. Physiological studies have proven that athletes with positive mental attitudes and average abilities often are formidable foes against a team of talented individuals with negative attitudes. **The world is teeming with people who practice sinking thinking.** They have the unique ability to always pull you down. Their whole perspective on life is clouded by only seeing or expecting things to "bottom out." Sinking thinkers embrace Murphy's Law, "Anything that can go wrong will go wrong."

If you want to rise to higher levels of fulfillment, peak performance and success, AVOID SINKING THINKING AT ALL COSTS. If you have been guilty of sinking thinking, and we all have at some point, decide today to eliminate sinking thinking thoughts, words, and phrases from your vocabulary.

Say goodbye to…I can't…I should have…I'm not good at…They won't let me…I would but…nobody will help me…That's impossible…I can't do that…I always do it this way…My situation is different…its been tried before…I don't have enough money…I'm too old…I'm too young...I didn't finish my education…I don't have the right look…They won't like it…They have already said no twice.

Power-Up To Power-Out

Nutrition experts agree that a hearty breakfast in the morning helps to boost your metabolism and your mental ability to process information. Schools across the country provide breakfast for students because numerous studies have documented that children learn better when they have eaten a nutritious breakfast.

This same principle applies to your mental attitude. On a daily basis we need to feed our minds a healthy diet of attitude strengthening and personal affirming information. This helps us build strong self-esteem, confidence, faith, and motivation. We get bombarded with negative things daily. We must take proactive measures to combat and detoxify ourselves from the effects of a negative environment. Watching, reading and listening to life affirming information is an excellent way to cleanse your thoughts.

Make every effort to fuel up on positive information. Take time to listen to positive music, or motivational messages. I have found reading aloud personal affirmations helps me tremendously. Doing so will strengthen your ability to maintain a positive attitude throughout the day. The ride or drive to and from work is a perfect time to power up.

Powering up should not be restricted to the daylight hours. Because your subconscious mind is always receptive to information, you can power up while you sleep. You can play music or messages while you sleep and your subconscious mind will receive and process the information. **Make the most of your mind by making the most of your time.**

I have even gotten my children involved in powering up to power out. Every morning before school, they say aloud who they are, who they will be, what they have, and what they can do. It's not surprising that both my daughters are performing above grade level. This is because we have instilled a can-do attitude in them, but first we had to instill a can-do attitude in ourselves. What are you instilling in your kids, students, or employees?

I have worked with schools to change their morning announcements into a time of proclaiming positive affirmations that have noticeable impacts on the student population. This same principle will work in the workplace as well. If you have a lounge or break room, put a motivational message on continuous play. Play different messages daily and watch the response. **Remember: If you tell yourself something long enough, eventually you will begin to believe it is true. If you believe something is true, your mind will motivate you to act on your beliefs.**

When The Dog Bites And The Bee Stings

Having a powered-up attitude does not prevent the unexpected from happening; although, it does provide you with the proper ammunition to combat the situation. There will be days when things will not go as planned. The best laid plans of mice and men often go awry. There are things that go bump in the night. There are circumstances that sneak up behind you and bite your buttocks. These are the days when the dog bites, and the bee stings.

During challenging situations, the big thinkers control their attitudes. You are the keeper of your peace of mind. You must be constantly aware that it is *your* mind and *your* peace that is being challenged. You are the only one who can allow someone or something to move you from a state of positive composure.

Undoubtedly there are some people who will go to great lengths to unsettle you. You do not have to succumb to their schemes or devices. The choice is totally yours how you will respond or react. To respond is to work at finding a solution to the problem. To react is to have an unproductive emotional response to a situation you are not helping to improve. **No one can change your positive attitude into a negative attitude without your permission and assistance.**

Time to pause and take action. If you don't already have an audio library of motivational and educational messages for powering up, now is the time to get one established. Get at least one message and listen to it daily. I have produced a special affirming tape entitled *Motivation for the Road Ahead*. You can also visit your local library or bookstore to find helpful materials.

Take Action to Succeed

In the back of this book you will find the complete list of affirmations I have provided at the beginning of each chapter. Take time to rewrite at least seven that address areas you want to address. By taking the time to write them you will reinforce the affirmations in your subconscious, this will help you when you begin to use them as part of your power-up to-power-out activities.

1.____

____

2.____

____

3.____

____

4.____

____

5.____

____

6.____

____

"For years I hung out with the chickens.
I thought I was a chicken
because I felt like a chicken.
When I finally realized that I was an eagle,
I packed my bags and said goodbye to my
chicken friends in the barnyard.
I have been soaring with the eagles ever since."

T. R. Williams
Speaker/ Author

I am better today than I was yesterday.
I'll be better tomorrow than I am today
and I have yet to give my best presentation.

Lesson Eight

Monitor Your Environment

We have been designed to adapt to our environment. Adaptation is a natural process which happens without being aware that it is happening. When you walk into a dark room and turn on the lights, your eyes immediately dilate to adjust to the brightness of the light. When your body gets too warm, you'll begin to perspire to cool off. These are natural bodily functions. You don't have to think about them; adjustments to the environment occur without conscious thought.

Your mind is your central control center. It will adapt to environmental surroundings in the same way your body adapts. Your environment is composed of all the things that influence your conscious and subconscious thoughts. **Everything around you is exerting influence on you daily, even though you may not be aware of the cumulative effects.**

Your mind is constantly receiving messages and impressions and relaying the information back to the control tower in your subconscious mind. Once that occurs, you automatically begin to act on the information. Your mind operates the same way a thermostat operates. It regulates how you think and act based on your mental temperature settings or beliefs. The key to breaking free from mental barriers, is to change your mental settings by setting them higher so you can expect more and achieve more.

This is a natural process. Your mind was designed to function this way. You are the product of your surroundings. Your thoughts, ambitions, and goals have all been impacted by your environment.

Who you are, what you are, and where you are in life can be credited to your environment. More importantly, who you will become and what you will achieve in the coming years will also be influenced by your environment. Mental adaptation is as natural as physical adaptation.

Practice Mind Control

To achieve the success that you desire, you must learn to protect yourself against negative influences caused by either your own actions or the actions of others. You must develop a mental immunity and low tolerance for negative people, negative places, and negative thoughts. Negative thoughts are trans-generational. They can be passed on from one generation to another just as easily as from one person to another. What kind of thoughts are you passing on?

When you release negative or destructive thoughts in your mind, you will impair your ability to be innovative and creative. Over the last decade, I have met and developed relationships with hundreds of incredibly successful people from many different walks of life. Without exception every one of them possesses the unique ability to be innovative or creative. Negative thoughts block the flow of creativity. The world is searching for creative, out-of-the-box thinkers. **Ordinary thinkers are a dime a dozen, creative thinkers are a rare find**.

When negative thoughts merge with negative emotions, they create a negative personality which will repel people from you. You could be repelling the very people you need to assist you. No one can become successful without assistance. At many points along your journey, you will need help. However, if you are perceived as a negative person, people will shy away from you and proceed to offer assistance elsewhere.

When negative thoughts are allowed to take root in your mind, eventually they will erode your character. They can mutate you into a totally different person. The world is full of people who are nursing negative thoughts from ten and twenty years ago. They have been robbed of peace of mind, joy, and a fulfilling life because a negative thought has been allowed to take root.

As long as you harbor negative thoughts about someone, you allow that person to occupy valuable space in your mind. When you let go of the grudges you have been holding, you free your hands to do more important things.

Garbage In, Garbage Out

All dreams, desires, and goals in life begin as thoughts. **Your words and thoughts are the containers that carry your future.** You have set your sights on achieving a higher level of success. You have the power to guard and dominate your thoughts. Whatever thoughts you allow to germinate and grow will determine your future. You hold the key to deciding how you want your life to be. If you fail to control your thoughts, you will live a life at the mercy of destructive forces.

Anyone who has experienced success has learned how to master thoughts even in the middle of challenges. **If in your mind you allow garbage to creep in, you will experience life on the garbage heap.** Avoid gossiping and engaging in petty issues. They pollute your mind and hinder your ability to think clearly and creatively.

Birds of a Feather Flock Together

Because we understand how the brain functions, we can use this natural process to catapult us forward instead of allowing it to push us back. Association brings about assimilation. The more you associate with something or someone, the more you will adapt or adopt their thinking, attitudes, and ambitions.

Attitudes and ambitions are transferable. They can be passed on. If you associate with sinking thinkers, eventually your thinking will begin to sink. If you associate with people who have big dreams and goals, your dreams and goals will begin to expand. It is a natural process, so use it for your benefit.

Practice these points:

1. **Always be aware of your environment**. Don't allow yourself to be in an atmosphere that is not conducive to growth and productivity. Monitor the information that you hear and see. Remember your subconscious mind is receiving information all the time. Keenly monitor what may be entering your mind consciously or subconsciously. Avoid at all cost people who have a negative outlook on life and low level ambitions, goals, or dreams.

2. **Get wise counsel from wise people.** Once you change your direction in life, there will always be people who will try to get you to turn back on your journey to your destiny. Don't let them influence your decision to advance in life. Everyone will *not* be supportive. Often your decision to change will conflict with their decision to remain the same.

   Seek wise counsel from wise individuals who are going where you want to go, doing what you want to do, and living a life you want to live. Spend time talking to people who have experienced success. Draw wisdom and knowledge from their successes and their failures. By learning from their experiences, you can increase the speed of your advancement.

   Much wisdom can be found between the pages of self-improvement books, biographies of successful people, and other publications. There is a treasure chest of free information at your local library; use it for your benefit. At the back of this book, I have provided a list of books that will help you with your transformation.

3. **Form partnerships for progress.** I discussed earlier how association brings about assimilation. Leave the chickens in the barnyard and seek out the eagles. Begin to associate with other people who want to be successful. Iron sharpens iron. If your want to be sharp, associate with sharp people. If you associate with dull people, you will be a dull person.

   Don't be hesitant about seeking out your partners for progress. When big thinkers perceive that you are serious about maximizing your potential, you will not have a problem finding people who will assist you along your journey. Some individuals may serve as your partners for a specific season in your life. Other partners for progress may serve as life-long mentors and friends.

4. **Make new friends in new social circles.** Seek out people who are balanced mentally, emotionally, and spiritually. Choose friends who will encourage you to maximize your potential and will support your efforts. Identify an organization where you can help ignite the power to succeed in others. Get to know the members and become active in the organization. When you cheerfully assist others, what you give will find its way back to you.

5. **Set high standards.** Regardless of your current status or state in life, decide to elevate yourself to a higher level of productivity, efficiency, advancement or purposeful living. Don't be happy or comfortable settling for second best. Develop a desire for excellence without excuses. Commit yourself to being a person with character and integrity. Meet project deadlines. Be an asset instead of a liability. Be on time. Shine your shoes. Organize your closet. Keep your car clean both inside and out. Tell the truth.

6. **Look important.** Don't leave home without looking like the person you want to be. Clothes don't make the person but they will surely introduce you from afar. Looking successful helps you to think and feel successful. How you look on the outside affects how you feel on the inside. Attention to hair and hygiene are equally important.

You can't go wrong in classic business attire with a necktie or scarf that reflects your personality. Avoid trendy colors and fashions. Select clothes that will transcend periodic style changes. Always make sure that your clothes are clean and wrinkle free before going out.

7. **Invest in improving yourself.** You can always do better than you are doing. There is always room for improvement in some aspect of your life. You can increase your vocabulary. Read a book every month. Become more health conscious and physically fit. Expand your understanding of the world around you. Strengthen your relationships. Spend more time in prayer. Mentor a student. Investing time and money in improving yourself or helping someone else is one of the best investments you can make.

8. **Live with an attitude of gratitude**. We often take too much for granted. If you have a place to live and food to eat, be grateful. If you are healthy and can think clearly, be grateful. If you have people who love and are concerned about you, be grateful. If you have an honest source of income, or the ability to get an education, be grateful. It is very easy to get caught up in the hustle and bustle of life and overlook our daily blessings.

   Often we spend a great deal of time focusing on what we don't have instead of appreciating what we do have. As you pursue success and fulfillment, take time to stop and smell the roses and count your blessings. Despite the challenges in your life, there are millions of people who would love to trade places with you.

Beating The Odds And Creating A Path

In the early nineties, I was selected to lead a public/private partnership effort to encourage local homebuilders to expand their focus to include the emerging first-time homebuyer market. During a visit to a new home sales office, I met Charles A. Thomas. Charles was selling homes to first-time homebuyers in a small residential community in southwest Houston. Charles was working for a homebuilding company that had created a new division for starter homes. He had been assigned to a community that was projected to be marginal at best in terms of projected sales.

Many of his clients were people who had limited savings, credit issues, or no credit history. They were hard working individuals who did not know what was required to purchase a home. Charles made it his mission to educate and facilitate the acquisition of homes for many people who never thought they would be homeowners. Despite the seemingly marginal client base and a sluggish economy, Charles began to experience success.

I recognized that Charles was very different from most salesmen catering to first-time buyers. He was smart and perceptive. He understood the psychology of selling homes and the psychology of dealing with customers. He made buyers feel valued and respected. I recognized that there were important things that Charles could teach me about being successful, even though he was working in an environment where he was expected to fail.

Charles and I began to talk regularly. To my surprise he was very liberal in sharing his challenges and his strategy for overcoming them.

As a member of the National Association of Homebuilders Sales and Marketing Council, he had become an expert in the business of marketing and selling homes. I was amazed that a person of his caliber, understanding, and experience was not the Sales Director of the company. He taught me valuable lessons by not allowing the low expectations and prejudice of others hinder his personal commitment to excellence and advancement. His daily affirmation is “I am better today than I was yesterday. I’ll be better tomorrow than I am today and I have yet to give my best presentation.”

During the following three years, Charles was the leading salesperson at the company. He broke all the sales projections and distinguished himself in the community. In 1996, his commitment to excellence motivated him to earn the honor of becoming a Member of the Institute of Residential Marketing (MIRM). It is the highest designation given by the National Association of Homebuilders in the new homes sales industry. He was the first African-American in the nation to earn this coveted designation.

In 1997, Charles received the National Sales Associate of the Year Award from the National Association of Real Estate Brokers. Despite his unprecedented accomplishments, Charles has never been offered the opportunities and recognition afforded other salespersons who hold high honors. Despite it all, Charles continues to pursue his goal of becoming a national training consultant assisting others to achieve a higher level of success in sales and marketing.

Shortly after we met, Charles and I were having lunch and he asked me a question that served to lift me to a higher level of achievement. He asked “What books have you read lately?”

I read magazines related to the homebuilding industry and marketing and sales. However, I felt I didn't have spare time for leisure reading. Charles explained that my thirst for knowledge and excellence could not end at MIT or Harvard. I had to continue investing in my future by reading books that could help me be more effective in all areas of my life, including business.

Charles began to tell me how important it was to read at least one book a month. He said that those who don't read are no better off than those who can't read. Charles made me commit to reading a book a month and developing a library. He encouraged me to visit used bookstores and buy great books at reduced prices. Charles directed me to read every book I bought and put its contents to work on my behalf.

I have kept my commitment. Reading at least one book a month has elevated my understanding and effectiveness as a leader, businessman, husband and father. The rewards of reading are too numerous to detail. It all began with me meeting a mentor, friend, and history maker, Charles A. Thomas.

Time to pause and take action. Always remember you are responsible for monitoring your mental and physical environment. Daily you should practice controlling your thoughts and defending your mind from the negative and self-defeating attacks. Maintain your passion to progress by powering-up to power-out. Do things that increase possibilities and promote success and purposeful living.

Take Action to Succeed

Revisit each of the eight points listed above. For each point commit yourself to doing at least one activity to enhance your life in each category. Establish a time frame for implementing or accomplishing each item you list. Later go back and write the date you achieved it.

1.____

____

2.____

____

3.____

____

4.____

____

5.____

____

6.____

____

7.____

____

8.____

____

"The way to success:
First have a clear goal, not a fuzzy one.
Sharpen this goal until it becomes specific and clearly defined in your conscious mind.
Hold it there until,
by a process of spiritual and intellectual osmosis it seeps into your unconscious.
Then you will have it because it has you.
Surround this goal with positive thoughts and faith.
Give it positive follow through.
This is the way success is achieved."

Norman Vincent Peale
Minister/Speaker/Author

Today I will review my goals, revisit my plans, assess my progress, and keep moving forward.

Lesson Nine

Chart Your Course of Action

If you don't know where you are going in life, any road will lead you there. Life-long success does not happen by accident. The actions you take today *will* determine the possibilities of your tomorrow. It's time to chart your course to a brighter future.

Establish a Reason to Succeed

The first step in charting your course of action is to establish a reason why you must succeed. You must identify a reason "why" you can't afford for certain aspects of your life to remain unchanged. Your reason "why" is very important. Without an unwavering reason "why," you will get sidetracked when you face obstacles that are sure to challenge you. Without an unwavering reason "why," you may allow someone to talk you out of achieving the success you deserve. Without an unwavering reason "why," you may change your focus and goals every three months and never accomplish anything.

Your reason "why" must be so strong that failure is not an option. Your reason "why" must be so strong that it becomes a part of the fiber of your soul. Your reason "why" must rise with you in the morning and go to bed with you at night. Your reason "why" must be a constant companion for the rest of your life.

Those who are stagnant in life have hundreds of reasons why they cannot succeed. All a successful person needs is one reason why he can. **The strength of your "why" will determine how high you will fly**.

As you are considering your reasons "why" you *must* go to the next level, consider the consequences of unfulfilled potential. Everyone has been given special abilities and desires; however, your commitment to maximize your potential is determined by the strength of your "why." Your reason "why" will require you to make adjustments in your life.

Sometimes making adjustments can be a difficult task. Remember that when the need to change outweighs the need to remain the same, you will make the necessary adjustment to change. Don't succumb to doubt, fear or apathy. Your future is at stake!

I have shared the story of how my acceptance at MIT opened the way for my classmates and other students at PVAMU. If I had changed my mind or my "why" for attending MIT, I would have jeopardized the academic advancement of others who were watching me.

How many people are watching your life? How many people are depending on you to lead the way? How many people are hoping you are the one who will create the path or break the barrier? How will your family be affected if you fail to fulfill your purpose? How will technological advances be delayed if you don't develop your invention? How many millions of dollars will you forfeit if you don't write that business plan, make that telephone call, build that relationship, or go the extra mile?

It is essential that you give birth to the hopes and aspirations that have been placed in you. Be committed to making your dreams become reality. Don't let them fall by the wayside. It's a tragic thing to abort your God-given potential by failing to establish a strong reason "why" you must succeed.

Create a Blueprint for Your Future

One of the most enjoyable aspects of my years as a real estate developer was designing the homes I built. My business partner, Chuck Stanton, and I would spend numerous hours exploring ways to make our homes showplaces of masterful design. Regardless of the size or sales price, we labored over every single aspect of the residence. When prospective buyers called the sales office to get directions to our subdivision, I would suggest they bring an oxygen tank because opening the doors to our homes would take their breath away.

To insure our vision would become reality, we developed a blueprint for every home we designed. The blueprint is the set of detailed instructions for how every component of the house is to be constructed or installed. By following instructions on the blueprint, each worker who is assisting our vision to become reality knows exactly what he should do to complete our vision. **Without a plan you cannot stand; without vision you will not complete the mission.**

I would never dump a pile of lumber on a residential lot and tell a framing crew to " just do the best you can at building us a house." Our vision was too important to leave to chance.

The blueprint directs the plumbers where to put the sinks, bathtubs, and commodes. Our house would not function as planned if the plumbers decided to put the commode in the kitchen and the electricians decided to put the oven in the bathroom. Without a blueprint we would have no way of knowing how the finished product would look.

Examine Your Priorities

Before I would begin to design a house, I would establish clear priorities for the levels of importance of specific design objectives. I had to set some boundaries for the way I wanted to achieve the goals. **When you design the plan for your future, it is important to develop your vision or blueprint based on clear priorities.**

As I meet young people who are committed to being successful, I am often informed that most of them don't have a clear set of priorities by which they govern their activities. As a result, far too many success minded individuals lose their way in the process of climbing up the ladder of success. In many instances the lack of clear priorities contributes to their demise. Regardless of your present status or position, you will benefit from establishing and revisiting clear priorities.

Without clear priorities or boundaries, it is easy for the desire for riches, fame, and influence to cloud your commitment to those whose lives you influence the most. How many individuals have mentally abandoned their spouses and children in pursuit of their career? What good are position and money, if you have alienated the people who support and love you.

Honesty, integrity, and character are still the hallmarks of greatness. If your commitment to advancement is so strong that you will lie, steal, cheat, and use people merely as tools to attain success, it's time to rethink your priorities. Regardless of your success or achievements, you still will feel like a failure.

Remember that money and fame are not substitutes for peace of mind. What good is success without peace of mind. You cannot have peace when you have sacrificed your soul on the altar of success. Your unregulated desire for success can become a curse rather than a blessing. The carnage of wounded, demoralized, stressed, and disoriented individuals will be a testament to your misdirected priorities.

There are countless individuals who have spent their entire adult lives chasing the "golden ring," only to realize that most of the things that bring internal peace and fulfillment are the simple things in life that were ignored. Don't wait for a tragic accident, divorce, death of a loved one, lay-off, or crash in the stock market to serve as your wake up call. Learn from the experiences of others and profit from their mistakes. We all need balance in our lives.

If you are married or have children, it is absolutely essential that you set boundaries in your life and your relationships with others. Today, more than ever the social structure of our society is under assault. The divorce rate is approaching fifty percent. The challenges facing our children are beyond belief. Regardless of whether they verbalize this or not, your children need your active participation in their lives. Your spouse and family need to be active participants in your goals, dreams and desire for success.

There is no substitute for the time you spend with your family. Your commitment to your family is measured in time spent with them rather than in your position, title, the size of your home, the type of car you drive, the events you attend, or the awards you receive. Don't get caught up in the illusion of success. **True success is achieved when at the end of the day, all those whose lives you have influenced have been enhanced by your success.**

I entered the corporate environment after graduating from MIT. Before I realized it I was being pulled in many directions by the obligations of my job. I was not prepared for the onslaught of evening meetings, social functions, late nights and weekends spent at the office. With each promotion or new position, I realized that I had to establish priorities and boundaries for how I was going to achieve success in my life and in the workplace**. If you don't establish your priorities, others will establish them for you.** I set up priorities according to five separate areas:

1. **God** - Will this negatively impact my personal relationship with Him?
2. **Myself** - Will this be detrimental to my mental, spiritual, or physical well being?
3. **My family** - Will my family suffer or benefit because of this decision?
4. **My job** - Will my ability to perform my job be positively or negatively affected?
5. **My friends and others** - Proper time and attention will be given to others but not at the expense of my other priorities?

Your priorities may be different from mine. It is important that you give serious consideration to what is of greatest value to you.

Also consider what price you are willing to pay to see your vision become reality. Every person who maximizes their potential will pay a price to do so. By establishing your priorities now, you can avoid getting caught up in the whirlwind or illusions of success. Priorities will help you manage your time and activities successfully. Once you establish your priorities, it's time to develop your goals.

Develop Achievable Goals

A vision without a method of implementation leads to great frustration. Once you have developed a vision of what you want to accomplish in your life, then it's time to develop a blueprint for the vision. Your blueprint will be your detailed instructions and timelines for seeing your vision become reality. The blueprint for your future consists of the goals and tasks required to see your vision become reality. Your goals will serve as daily motivation for persevering. You will find that your goals will energize you. Many people find new strength by identifying a goal and giving their full measure to accomplish the goal.

Your determination to achieve your goals must be as strong as your reason "why." As your goals become a positive obsession, they will automatically begin to provide the inspiration needed to accomplish peak performance and advancement. Once you become totally committed to achieving your goals, they become embedded in your subconscious. When this occurs, your subconscious begins to act on cruise control. You will begin to automatically respond in a way that supports achievement of your goals.

Every goal should have a specific timeline associated with its anticipated completion. Remember Rome was not built in a day. The ultimate inspiration is a timeline. The achievement of a goal is a process. The price of success must be made in daily installments. Day-by-day and step-by-step you will draw closer to achieving your goals.

Begin to examine everything you do by asking yourself the question, "How will this help me achieve my goal or fulfill my purpose?" If you cannot answer positively, then consider better uses of your time and resources. Life is too short and time is too valuable to be engaged in unproductive activities.

Start by establishing your long-term goals. Where do you want to be five, ten and twenty years from now? What type of impact do you want to be making on your family, your company, your career, and your finances? What type of impact do you want to have on your community, your state, the nation? Where do you want to be living and vacationing? What charities, organizations or social causes do you want to be supporting. Your goals will require time and preparation to achieve. **Goals are your destination points on your way to fulfilling your destiny.**

Once you have established your destination points, then it's time to determine the route you will take to arrive at your destination. The road to your destination is paved with numerous short-term goals. These are goals that can be accomplished within a two year period. Identify activities that must be accomplished in each month of the year. Having a partner for progress to assist you in this may be helpful. Each month should have action items for each week. Each week should have action items for each day.

Many years ago my wife and I were encouraged to set yearly goals for different aspects of our life. At that time I had never considered that by doing this I could magnetize my family to attract unforeseen favor, wealth, and promotion. However, we followed the instructions and without fail, the goals we established were achieved. New Year's Eve has become our time of great thanksgiving for all our exceeding blessings and a time of great anticipation to watch how God will prove Himself faithful during the coming year. How do you spend New Year's Eve? Is it helping you achieve your goals?

Assess Your Progress

Goals require constant attention to ensure their completion. On a periodic basis you should assess your progress toward achieving your goals. Revisiting your goals daily will keep them embedded in your subconscious mind and also allow you to gauge your progress. Make use of a personal daily planner. Post a monthly calendar with your goals for each day of the week clearly visible. Progress is the optimum word. **Don't confuse motion with progress.**

During this time of transformation, you must be committed to making *progress* toward achieving your goals. If you encounter unforeseen challenges, you may have to make a detour. Sometimes the shortest distance between your two points is a crooked line. Understand that detours will be necessary along the way. Although you may have to change the path you travel, always keep your destination as your target. Avoid getting sidetracked with time consuming, resource depleting activities that blur your focus.

Consider this point. If I select New York City as my destination, I can drive my car, I can take a bus, I can take a train, I can fly in an airplane, or I can take a boat. The airplane is the fastest mode of travel. However, if I have to take a bus and stop in every town along the way, my destination will still be New York City.

If my bus makes a stop in Nashville, Tennessee and after getting off to stretch my legs, I mistakenly board the wrong bus, I will have to make some mid-course corrections. I must exit the bus as soon as I recognize I'm headed in the wrong direction. Sometimes you may think the path you are traveling will lead to your destination until you realize that you have been misdirected. At the point you become aware of your situation, do whatever is necessary to get back on track and keep moving forward.

Time to pause and take action. Here is your opportunity to establish your vision. It is not enough only to talk about what you want to accomplish. You must clearly articulate your vision on paper.

Taking Action to Succeed

Write goals you want to accomplish in the long term and the short term. Be specific. Establish a realistic timeline for achieving your goals. What you write will serve as your blueprint for your next level of success and personal fulfillment. Avoid the temptation to take this exercise lightly. Your future is literally in your hands.

My long-term goals are....... I would like to achieve them in ....

1.____

____

2.____

____

3.____

____

My short-term goals are...... I would like to achieve them in ......

1.____

____

2.____

____

3.____

____

For verily I say to you
whoever shall say to this mountain,
move and go into the sea;
and shall not doubt in his heart,
but believes
those things he says shall come to pass,
he shall have whatever he says.
...whatever things you desire when you pray
believe that you have them
and you will have them

Jesus Christ
Mark 11:23-24

I am building my new reality with the words that I speak and visions I see. My best is yet to come.

Lesson Ten

Create Your Future

You have two very powerful tools that can be used to accelerate the speed at which your transformation occurs. You can use the power of your words and the power of your mind or thoughts to literally create a new reality and a brighter future. I, along with numerous other successful individuals, have used these two tools to catapult us to a new level of productivity in the workplace, earn higher incomes, increase academic performance, and find personal fulfillment and peace of mind. As you discipline yourself to use these tools daily, expect to experience a quantum leap in what will materialize for you.

Speak Your Future into Reality

Words have tremendous power. You can change the atmosphere of a situation with the words you speak. Words that you speak will impact you as well as others around you. What you say will have a significant impact on what will materialize for you, because words have creative power. When you speak words, your whole physical being responds to them. It is important to control the words you speak. Say the things that you want, and avoid speaking words of doubt, fear, failure, sickness, and poverty. **Only speak the things you want even if you don't know how you are going to get them.**

The fact that I am a national speaker, author, and trainer is the result of me speaking words even though I did not know *exactly* how it was going to occur. When I left the corporate real estate industry, many of my corporate friends thought I was having an early mid-life crisis. I had just completed obtaining the building permits for a 15 million dollar office building in west Houston. The leasing campaign was underway and construction was about to begin.

Before I made my decision to leave, I considered the possibility of moving into senior management positions that included training for large real estate companies. I thought it would be a perfect fit. I sent up trial balloons to examine my possibilities. The response from numerous executive recruiters was less than positive.

They said companies are looking for an executive with years of experience in training. While 13 years in corporate real estate managing sales, development and construction and a Masters degree from MIT was impressive, I did not fit their limited view of what large real estate companies were looking for. I realized that if I left my corporate position so that I could expand the impact I have on individuals and organizations, there was no turning back.

I was convinced that if I developed a logical plan and kept speaking only what I wanted, eventually it would materialize for me. The challenge was holding my course until I arrived at my destination. I was often tempted to say negative things based on how the situation appeared. I had to daily walk by faith and not by sight. However, over time things began to change. I began to get invitations from conferences, corporations, schools and colleges. The response to my presentations was overwhelming. There was no question about whether I had made the right decision.

May I Have Your Order, Please

Every time you verbalize negative or debilitating thoughts, you undermine and delay your advancement. Tragically, many of us are programmed to speak negative words, unconsciously unaware of the detrimental effects they are having on our lives.

Proverbs 18:12 states that death and life are in the power of the tongue. Your words have creative power. You can create a new reality for yourself by controlling and positively directing your words. You can talk your way into sickness and disease just as easily as you can talk yourself into health and wholeness. You can talk your way into poverty and lack or success and fulfillment. You can build people up or tear someone down with the words of your mouth. The choice is up to you how you direct the power of your tongue.

Your spoken words have power to fulfill their potential. Remember, "What you say is what you get." Don't say anything you don't want to materialize in your life. I often hear people say things like, "My kids are driving me crazy," or "This job is about to kill me," and I immediately in a caring way encourage them to rephrase their statements. Successful people develop a habit of speaking only positive words about their future.

I'm sure you have visited a fast-food restaurant with a drive-through window. You place your order by speaking into the voice box near the menu board. Once you place your order, you drive around to the window and pick up your order. The items you requested are handed to you in a bag. Be careful what you order because it will be handed to you.

You have a television in your home. Most viewers don't understand all the working and science of telecommunication transmission. All you know is that you plug it in, turn it on, and from invisible rays traveling through the air, an image appears on your television screen.

How and what happens in the unseen realm is not all clear to me, but what is clear is that there is an eternal principle that what you say is what you get. You don't have to know how or why it works to use it to your benefit; just do it consistently.

If your heart's desire is to do something that no one else has done, in your family, in your workplace, or in your industry, then you are going to have to consistently and deliberately speak words that are in agreement with your desires. If your goal is to rise to a higher level of success professionally, to be exceptional, to step out of the crowd, then you will have to speak it into reality. You will need to say:

"I am an exceptional manager. No matter what the rest of the teams are doing, I have the ability to motivate my team to achieve what no other team in the company has been able to achieve."

Even though at this point you may not be a manager, if your goal is to be a manager, then speak words that are in agreement with your desire. You need to say:

"I have those characteristics within me to be successful and I will not settle for being average. I will go beyond the call of duty with joy. I am setting myself apart from the crowd and daily others are recognizing the greatness in me."

When you speak affirming words on a daily basis, subconsciously things will begin to happen that act as a magnet to draw you to the things you desire. Continuous repetition is the key. By saying things again and again the new information will enter and be stored in your subconscious, creating a new image of who you are and what you can do. During this time of transformation, commit yourself to the life-long process of daily speaking only those things you want to become reality in your life.

Visualize Your Future into Reality

You can change your reality by visualizing what you want. Your brain has the unique ability to create vivid mental pictures on the screen of your imagination. **The mind does not know the difference between that which is imagined from that which is real.** Consider this point. Have you ever had a dream and in the dream you were in a stressful situation and you began to run? Although you were still sleeping, your body began to respond to the experience you were having in your mind. Maybe your breathing pattern changed, or you began to move or speak out. Even though this was not an actual experience, your mind was having an experience. Therefore, your body reacted.

Your mind is as malleable as clay. If you take a quarter and press it in the clay, when the quarter is removed the imprint of the coin remains in the clay. Your mind is equally as flexible and malleable as clay when you apply the principle of visualization. Visualization is an important and vital tool for catapulting you to the next level of success you desire. Use it daily to reinforce the mental pictures of those things you desire.

Visualization is applicable to every aspect of your life to achieve professional advancement, enhance personal relationships, increase academic performance, and experience financial prosperity.

This principle works for the young and the young at heart, from senior vice presidents to senior citizens, from athletes to administrators. In my sessions I have seen the full gambit of individuals successfully employ this principle. **Visualize your new reality on the screen of your vivid imagination.**

Research has proven that the mind can achieve dominating thoughts, directing the body to carry out the vivid images of performances as if they had already been accomplished and were being reenacted.

If you are an athlete and you want to improve your performance, begin to visualize yourself executing the play flawlessly. If you are a senior vice president who has to make a presentation to the board of directors or a potential client, visualize yourself walking into the room with confidence and making the winning presentation.

Maybe you are an educator. You must visualize yourself walking into a room of students. See yourself connecting with the students and watching the lights in the eyes of those students begin to shine. If you are an underachiever or a small thinker, you must see yourself rising to the top by maximizing your potential.

Maybe you are a husband and father. Visualize yourself being a husband who appreciates and understands his wife. See yourself being a loving and patient father who enjoys spending time with his kids, teaching them how to be the best they were created to be.

Using words, visual images and emotions simulate each experience just as if it were actually occurring. If you are about to go into a meeting, take a test or participate in an athletic event, take time to visualize yourself executing the activity flawlessly. After the event take time to analyze or access your performance. If you did well, reinforce your accomplishment by saying, I did great and next time I'll do even better. If you did not perform at your maximum level tell yourself, this was not my best and next time I'll do much better.

When you envision a brighter future, the things you visualize will leave a powerful imprint on your mind. Subconsciously your mind and your body will respond to cause it to become reality in your life. Use your five senses to enhance your ability to mentally experience the thing you desire. Not only should you visualize it, take it to a higher level and imagine feeling it, tasting it, smelling it as you experience the emotion of your vision.

This principle has worked for me on countless occasions and it will work for you. At my first job in Boston, I put this principle to work. On my cubical wall I posted pictures of prominent individuals who were involved in construction or real estate development in the Boston area. My goal was to become familiar with their names, faces and companies.

Before I left Boston, three years later, I had developed a professional relationship with all but one person whose picture was on my wall. One of the men on the wall became the Regional Vice President for a company that was opening an office in Houston. He hired me to fill the position of Executive Director, my income almost doubled. At the time I put those pictures on my wall, I had no idea how my life would be influenced by such a simple act.

Paid In Full

When my wife and I decided it was time to get out of debt we used this strategy again. We listed all of our creditors and bills (which were numerous). We posted them on the wall in our kitchen. We had over 40 listings of debts that needed to be paid. On a daily basis we began to speak to the list of bills and say that each one was being paid.

When we started, we had no idea how we were going to pay the items on the list. We began to imagine ourselves debt-free. We imagined walking up to the list and drawing a line through each listing as it was paid. We attended seminars on how to get out of debt. We read books on how to save money, and we prayed that God would help us get out of the terrible financial mess we had created for ourselves.

Almost immediately, money began to come from unexpected sources, creditors agreed to significantly reduce our outstanding balances if we agreed to pay the adjusted balance. It was during this period that one creditor canceled a $95,000 debt. Within two years we had paid off everything on the list except our home.

Lights, Camera, Action

When I decided to produce my first television series, I repeated this principle. I wanted to produce a ten-part television series on everything you need to know about the home buying process. When I was selling homes, I met scores of people who had no clue of what was required to get a mortgage for a home.

I wanted to create a television program that would help them avoid making mistakes that would hinder their ability to purchase a home now or in the future.

Although I had extensive radio experience, I was a professional radio announcer in college and had produced several radio talk shows in Houston, I had no television experience. I have never let the fact that I have not done something before be a deterrent to me doing anything I wanted to do. I typed the name of the series and the topic of each program in the series and posted the list in my office. I had no sponsors, no television studio, no crew, and no channel to air the series.

I began to study television shows with a different level of intensity. I started visiting television studios and talking to directors of programming for television stations. I started visualizing myself talking into the camera and interviewing guests. I developed a marketing strategy for presenting the concept to potential sponsors and began calling anybody I thought might be remotely interested in participating. Two months later, I had secured sponsors, a studio, a crew, and a station to air the series. The series became one of the highest rated programs at the station. Dare to dream the impossible dream. **You have to see it in your mind before you can see it with your eyes and touch it with your hands.**

I had such a great time with the television program that I have decided that I would like to host several national television specials. I can reach a much larger audience by using television as a vehicle for sharing these and other principles for transforming lives. I believe it's only a matter of time before it becomes a reality.

Time to pause and take action. You have the tools in your mouth and your mind to recreate your life. Use these tools to your advantage. The more you use them the greater the impact will be. During this time of transformation, begin to surround yourself with visual images of what you want your life to reflect. Get books, magazines, videotapes, pictures, and posters so that you can constantly make imprints in your mind of what you want to become reality for you. Visit places that are examples of what you want to experience in your life.

Close your eyes and imagine yourself doing things you have not done. Close your eyes and see yourself going where you have not gone. Close your eyes and see yourself just as you want to be. Daily repetition is the key to getting maximum results. **You do not have to know how it will all come together at the time you *start* to visualize your future.** Visualizing your future does not cost you anything but time and your commitment to stay on course until your vision becomes reality. **Knowledge is not power; acting on your knowledge produces power**.

Taking Action to Succeed

Write down exactly what you want to speak into reality regarding your future. Consider these categories: your job, finances, relationships, personal goals, where you want to live, what you want to drive, places you want to vacation, other people you want to positively influence.

1. My education, job or career ______________________________
____

2. My relationships______________________________________
____

3. My personal goals______________________________________
____

4. I would like to live in __________________________________
____

5. I would like to earn an income of _______________________
____

6. I would like to financially support ________________________
____

7. I will be a positive influence in the life/lives of ______________
____

**"Whenever I make a decision
to use my natural attributes, abilities,
and ambitions to honor God,
I activate the supernatural power,
presence and protection of God
to help me be successful."**

T. R. Williams
Speaker/ Author

God I thank you that you are my constant companion
on my journey through life.
You are my source of power, ability, and influence.

Lesson Eleven

How to get Supernatural Results in a Natural World

I am often asked why or how do I manage to have such a lasting impact on the lives of people who here me speak. Even though the reaction and results are the same where ever I speak, it still amazes me. At times the outpouring of appreciation becomes overwhelming. I never get tired of people telling me how their lives were positively impacted by my presentations.

In this lesson, I will share with you how I get supernatural results in a natural world. What I am about to discuss may seem a bit farfetched to some and uncomfortable for others, but for those who are committed to experiencing a new level of fulfillment, let me share my secret with you.

Let me begin by covering some of the primary elements for understanding how man is designed to function. Man is a tripartite being, meaning he is made of three parts. Man is a spirit. He possesses a soul, and he occupies a body. You are a spiritual being having an earthly experience in a physical body.

Each of us is composed of these three parts. Most of us have a working knowledge of how the body functions; however, considerably less attention is given to the spirit and soul aspects.

The key to having supernatural results in a natural world is understanding the needs and abilities of the body, soul, and spirit.

1. **The Body** is the temporary physical dwelling place for the spirit during its assignment on earth. The body requires proper nutrition, rest, and exercise to remain in a maximized state. At the point the body ceases to function properly, the spirit and soul must vacate and return to the supernatural realm.

2. **The Soul** is comprised of the mind, the will, the imagination, the emotions and the intellect. Your soul is the control center for everything you choose, everything you think, and everything you feel. All of your mental abilities are connected to your soul. Your values and beliefs reside in your soul.

3. **The Spirit** is the eternal essence of man. It is the aspect of man that can transcend into the realm of the supernatural. The spirit of man is born in the mind of God. It is your connection to the power and presence of the forces of good and evil. The spirit gives life and animation to the physical body.

The first step to understanding how to get supernatural results in a natural world is to understand that **you function according to the established laws of two realms, the natural realm and the supernatural or spirit realm.** The natural realm is composed of things that you can detect with your five senses. The supernatural realm is composed of the source and forces of life and the substance by which all material things exist. Although the supernatural realm cannot be seen with the human eye, it is real and has a tremendous influence on how you live your life.

Grounded For Life

We are all familiar with the law of gravity. This unseen force exerts a pull on all objects within the earth's atmosphere. The unseen force of gravity keeps us grounded to the earth. The law of gravity operates 24 hours a day, 7 days a week, 365 days a year. Whether you are aware of its operation or not, you are still subject to its force. **Whether you personally believe in gravity or not, does not influence its power.** It is impossible to decide to live your life outside the force of gravity. Despite your educational background, financial status, or personal commitment. As long as you live on the earth you will be subject to the law of gravity.

When I was a child I loved jumping off the roof of our one-story home. I loved the feeling of quickly descending to the ground. Every time I jumped off the roof I always went downward. If I jumped off in the morning, I went downward. If I jumped off in the evening, I went downward. Even when I flapped my arms like a bird, I went downward. My thoughts and actions had no influence on the force of gravity.

The law of gravity is unchanging. It is constant and under normal conditions, its force is beyond escape. Everything that man designs for operation on the earth assumes that the force of gravity will remain the same. However, if the force of gravity ever disappeared, life on the planet would be completely disrupted and absolute chaos would ensue. We could float into space.

The established laws of the supernatural or spiritual realm are more powerful and constant than the force of gravity. They supercede natural laws and are unchanging in their application.

Spiritual laws daily exert an unseen influence over our lives. The spiritual laws have been established by God. The unseen forces of good and evil operate according to these established supernatural laws.

The key to getting supernatural results in a natural world is increasing your understanding of the spiritual laws and applying them to every aspect of your life. I have found that the greatest source of spiritual laws for successful living are found in the Bible.

Let's Get Personal

When I was growing up, I thought that God was some cosmic Creator who caused people to get sick and die. He sent floods, storms, earthquakes, and tornadoes. That was why they were called "acts of God." God served as the gatekeeper to heaven and hell and decided where people would spend eternity.

As I began to look for success principles to transform my life, I kept hearing sayings that were attributed to the Bible. I was so committed to changing my life that I would read anything that could possibly hold some truths that could help me to a new level of success and fulfillment.

I tapped into the eternal power source by developing a personal relationship with the Creator of the universe through the teaching of the Bible. At first it was hard to comprehend how an all knowing, all powerful, eternal, omnipresent Spirit could be concerned about me.

There are over six billion people in the world. How could I matter to the Creator of six billion people? Then I read that His awesome knowledge is so vast that the hairs on my head are numbered, even though the number changes every time I comb my hair! Every star in every galaxy has been named by the Creator, and yet He desires to have a *personal* relationship with all six billion of us.

The God Space

Each one of us has been designed with a special void or empty space in our being. This space is sometimes referred to as the "God Space." It's a place in our spirit designed exclusively for the Master Creator to occupy.

I am the proud father of two wonderful daughters. Although they are separate from me, they both contain a part of me. They bear a physical resemblance to the source from which they came. I have permanently left my mark on their physical appearance. Wherever I go with my girls, people comment that there could never be any question as to who their father is because they clearly have a part of me in them.

My daughters had no choice in the matter of who their father would be and what part of me would be encoded in their lives. However, the Master Creator does not automatically occupy the space he has created for Himself. **God waits for an invitation from His creation to assume His rightful place in each life.** It's called "free choice." You are free to make the choice whether you will live your life with or without God's peace, power and protection in your life.

Many times because we lack understanding, we try to fill the "God Space" with other things, hoping we will experience fulfillment. Countless individuals have tried to fill the space with success, money, notoriety, sex, drugs, and alcohol, all to no avail. Nothing can be substituted for the space that only God can fill. Ultimate success and fulfillment can only be experienced when the Master Creator occupies His rightful place in the life of His creation. By developing a personal relationship with God, you tap into an unlimited knowledge and power source.

The Leading Edge

We all are born with talents and abilities; however, there are instances when your natural talents and abilities reach their limits. There are situations when natural education, intellect, and understanding are not sufficient. There are challenges that are insurmountable using your own strength and tenacity. That's when having the ability to draw from God's supernatural power gives you the leading edge. **The supernatural knowledge and power from God enables you to accomplish what you could not accomplish with your own ability, influence, or intelligence.**

I recognize that for many people this is a very sensitive subject; however, I would be remiss in my responsibilities if I did not share with you how to experience a supernatural life in this natural world. Maybe you are at a point in your life where you have tried to find fulfillment, and yet you sense something is missing. If you want to know the one thing that will make your transformation truly life-changing, it is developing a personal relationship with the Master Creator, the giver of life and purpose.

By following His spiritual laws for abundant life, you can experience a higher level of living and fulfillment beyond comprehension. However, I must inform you that there is a significant price to pay for following God's laws for living. It requires living a life of constant reliance on His help and direction. Most people, especially those who are successful, pride themselves on being "self-reliant." But at some point "self-reliance" will reach its limitations, then what do you do? Where do you go? Who can you call on for help in your time of need?

To get the supernatural results requires a lifestyle of being continuously connected to the supernatural power source. It's the difference between being plugged into an electrical socket or operating on batteries. At some point the batteries will get weak and become powerless, but the electrical socket provides a consistent unending source of power.

Throughout this book I have made references to spiritual aspects of my life. I have done this out of necessity. It would be impossible to honestly share with you the events in my life and not mention how divine intervention and direction have made all the difference in my ability to succeed and experience fulfillment.

I wish I could say that my educational background alone is the source of my success, but I cannot. There are hundreds of thousands of highly educated individuals who are miserable and living defeated lives. I wish I could say that my strong will and unwavering determination to make it happen was the single source of my success, but I cannot. There are scores of people who were determined, but just never saw their dreams become reality. Allow me to share a unique incident that will illustrate my point.

Tell The Storm To Cease

I conducted an eight-part seminar for a group of high school students who had been involved in unproductive and criminal activity. Because of their behavior they were placed in a boot camp type program. I was contacted because many of the students were not improving after being admitted to the program.

After the first session, I began to see significant changes in the attitudes of the students toward me and the information I was presenting. Many of the students were from families that were dysfunctional at best and many of the kids had experienced some form of continuous mental abuse. While the assignment was challenging to say the least, I spoke to the students from my heart and they soon realized I was there to help them become more than they ever dreamed they could be.

There was one young man who was totally adamant about not wanting to be a part of any of the discussions. He was rude and took every opportunity to contradict my principles for changing their course in life. After the second session, I had reached the end of my rope dealing with the young man. It was obvious that I was dealing with a very troubled young man. On the way home, I decided to pray for specific direction on how to reach him.

Approximately thirty minutes later I knew exactly what to do. I didn't understand it, but I knew I was supposed to look at the young man and tell the storm to cease. At the conclusion of the next meeting I asked the young man to step out into the hall because I wanted to talk to him privately. He reluctantly followed me out into the hall.

I looked him eye to eye and told him that his Creator was aware of what he had been through. I told him "I have specific instructions to tell the storm in your life to cease." Remember words have creative power. I had no idea how the young man would respond to this completely unorthodox interaction.

His countenance took on a strange puzzled look. I asked him had he ever been in a storm? He began to tell me that when he was younger a tornado came and picked up his family's mobile home and dashed it into a neighbors field. He and his mother were inside and were tossed around like rag dolls and found themselves underneath debris in the field. This young man knew what it was like to be in a storm.

After that conversation, the young man gave me his utmost respect during the remaining sessions. I received a letter from him letting me know how much he appreciated the time I spent teaching him how to change his course in life. The last paragraph of his letter ended saying " The storm has ended, thank you for caring."

While I often meet people after my sessions who feel as though I was addressing their particular situation, I don't ever recall having a personal message for anyone in my sessions. I did not know anything about the young man's past experiences before I spoke to him. He needed a divine supernatural intervention in his life from someone that had a power source greater than his own.

I am glad that I could call upon God to help me assist this young man. I don't think he will ever forget that life-changing experience, nor will he doubt that the Creator of the universe is very concerned about him.

Being spiritually connected to my Master Creator and His unlimited grace, knowledge and power really has made a tremendous difference in my life and my effectiveness as a speaker and trainer. He knows the needs of every person in the audience. He directs me what to say during the course of the presentation. Divine wisdom is available to me and I constantly draw from Him.

I am always aware that I am not transforming lives and organizations solely with my own ability. I have a supernatural partner in everything I do. It is easy to be a big thinker when God is your partner. He is very comfortable doing big things. My peace of mind and confidence are based on His word alone. **It is not difficult to have faith in your future when the One who holds your future is by your side**. He is helping me complete my earthly assignment and He's making it a fantastic journey.

Jesus said, "*I came that you might have life and that you have it more abundantly*" *John 10:10.* God wants us to live an abundant productive life through Christ. The way to do that is to become a recipient of His love, forgiveness, eternal presence and power. Jesus said, "*Ask and you shall receive, seek and ye shall find, knock and the door will be opened for you*" *Matthew 7:7.* This is an open invitation to make the spiritual connection to the giver of life and purpose. This is the path to getting supernatural results in a natural world.

Time to pause and take action. During this time of transformation, commit yourself to tightening your spiritual connection. The spiritual laws can work for you or against you. Take the time and effort to understand how they work. Principles for abundant living can be found in the pages of the Bible.

Taking Action to Succeed

Make sure your spiritual battery posts are not corroded and your cable wires are not shorted out. You want to insure there is nothing in your life to hinder the supernatural power of God that is available to you.

Sometime today find a quiet place away from the hustle and bustle, and consider the contents of this chapter. Ask yourself the following soul searching questions:

1. Do I have a personal relationship with my Creator? __________

____

2. How strong is my relationship?___________________________

____

3. Can it be strengthened?________________________________

____

4. Am I committed to making it stronger? ___________________

____

Take time to read the 8th and 28th chapters of Deuteronomy, it's found in the old testament of the Bible. These passages are quite revealing.

"To experience a fruitful life you cannot be content as a human being. You must become a human doing. For it is the "doing" that maximizes the "being."

T. R. Williams
Speaker/ Author

The fruit of my thoughts, dreams and ambitions reach maturity through the actions of my hands; therefore, I will never allow my hands to be idle.

Lesson Twelve

On Your Mark...Ready...Set... Grow !!!

In the preceding chapters, I have shared with you principles and life lessons that can transform losers into winners and small thinkers into big thinkers. Use these tools to learn more, earn more, achieve more, receive more, give more, and live more.

The journey of a thousand miles begins with the first step. As a result of reading each of the life-changing lessons and completing the exercises, you are well on your way. There is nothing mysterious or complicated about transforming your life. These lessons will work for anyone who will use them. The challenge we all face is whether we will act on the information. Remember knowledge is not power. Knowledge put into action is power. You have been given the tools to transform your life and the lives of those you influence. Now what will you do with it?

These lessons lifted me out of a stagnant state and elevated me and thousands of others, to new levels of success and fulfillment. There is an awesome freedom and infusion of energy that comes when you know you are living according to your purpose and experiencing success and fulfillment. Make the most of what you have learned. Before we conclude this time together, let me leave you with three powerful points for continuing your transformation.

Start Where You Are

There is no better time than the present to take action to move to the next level. No situation is beyond changing; don't procrastinate because things are not perfect. It's only when you start by taking action that things will change in your favor. Don't wait on anyone else before you make your move. Remember, there will always be people who will try to talk you out of your decision to change. Start right where you are. If you can't walk then crawl. The key is to move forward. If you can't run, then walk. Just be committed to pressing toward your goal. If you can't fly then run as fast as you can, but by all means keep moving forward. Your destiny awaits you, and the clock is ticking.

Use What You Have

Often it is easy to procrastinate by concentrating on what you don't have while ignoring what you do have. I have never had *everything* I needed when I set a goal, or started a project. You already have things that you need to *start* the process. Use what you have. If you look around you I'm sure you can find resources that are available to you. Be bold and ask for help from people who can assist you.

You already have skills, experiences, and knowledge to put you on the path to success. Your desires, talents, and abilities will create a place for you to succeed. However, you must be committed to fine-tuning and perfecting what you already possess. You can't afford to have an opportunity presented to you, and you are not fully prepared to seize it with both hands and feet.

Do What You Can

It has been said that opportunity only knocks once. I believe opportunity usually stands quietly by your side and waits to be recognized. Do what you can. The key word is "do." You must do something different if you want different results. This entire book is about doing something different to change your life. If you have a pulse and a functioning brain you can do something to advance your life. You can do something starting now and every day for the rest of your life to improve your life and the lives of others. Here are things you can do beginning right now.

39 Things You Can Do

1. You can reread this book

2. You can transform your life.

3. You can recondition your subconscious for success.

4. You can strengthen your desire to be successful and experience fulfillment.

5. You can control your thoughts.

6. You can counter negative thoughts with positive thoughts.

7. You can find your purpose in life.

8. You can embrace your unique purpose.

9. You can strengthen your self-esteem.
10. You can cause the seeds of your success to begin to grow.
11. You can list good attributes about yourself.
12. You can change.
13. You can move your "*but*" out of the way.
14. You can conquer your fears by taking action.
15. You can use your past failures as a springboard for success.
16. You can dispel every belief that limits your potential.
17. You can develop a confident attitude.
18. You can live with great expectations.
19. You can avoid sinking thinking.
20. You can control your emotions.
21. You can change your surroundings.
22. You can practice mind control.
23. You can think creatively.

24. You can monitor your environment.

25. You can establish a reason to succeed.

26. You can establish clear priorities.

27. You can create a blueprint for your future.

28. You can develop and achieve long-term goals.

29. You can develop and achieve short-term goals.

30. You can assess your progress.

31. You can create your future.

32. You can speak your future into reality.

33. You can visualize your future into reality.

34. You can get supernatural results in a natural world.

35. You can have a personal relationship with God.

36. You can start where you are.

37. You can use what you have.

38. You can do what you can.

39. You can recommend this book to someone else.

This is a time of birthing dreams and the season for maximizing your potential. The world is better because of the influence of progressive thinkers like you, people of purpose with positive self-esteem. Those who have overcome numerous challenges, fears, and failures with a confident attitude and have charted their courses for success.

Individuals just like you have created a new reality with the words of their mouths and visions in their minds and have experienced the desires of their hearts. You are a part of the bold breed who break through the barricades to success and race forward to reach for the unreachable, dream the impossible, and release all the potential that resides within.

Remember, you already possess the power to succeed. Now you have the principles to ignite your power. Your mind, your mouth, and your actions will determine how high you soar in life. Whether you are a civic leader, CEO, manager, educator, or student, you can realize a significant improvement in your life by implementing the strategies in this book. Whether you are a parent or a president, greater success and fulfillment are within your grasp.

I have been very honest and open about my transformation, I have spoken to you from my heart. With each word I wrote, I prayed that it would penetrate your heart and spirit. I believe that this book will be a continuing source of information and inspiration along your journey. You have so much to offer and so much to accomplish. It has been my sincere pleasure to spend this time with you. May you experience the abundant life as you trust God to do exceedingly, abundantly above anything you could ask or think as you acknowledge Him in everything you do.

As you experience transformations in your life, I want to hear about them. I am one of your partners for progress and I want to stay informed regarding your achievements. I want to hear your success stories as well as your challenges. Contact me at Eagles Wings Inc. 1749 Texas Parkway, Suite 180, Houston-Missouri City, Texas 77489 or e-mail: trwilliams@eagleswingsinc.com.

Share this information with other like-minded individuals. Form power groups and encourage each other to achieve new levels of success and fulfillment. Remember, this book is your tool to finding and fulfilling your divine assignment. Use each lesson as a catalyst for discussions in your management meetings, classrooms, or with your family and friends. There *is* more to life, and yes you can get supernatural results in a natural world. Seize the moment and experience the difference by ***Igniting the Power to Succeed***.

Power Points from T. R. Williams

The following 77 quotes from T. R. Williams have been assembled from the lessons in ***Igniting the Power to Succeed***.

1. Your mind is the soil from which a bountiful crop of new possibilities will emerge.
2. The thoughts of your mind are the flames that will ignite your personal power to succeed. Your thoughts and beliefs can also be fountains of hopelessness and despair that extinguish your potential and drown your possibilities.
3. Doubt is the combustible fuel of the power to fail.
4. Understanding who you are is the key that will free you from lower level thinking, lower level behavior, and lower level expectations.
5. The power of your mind is so vast that once you discover its ability, it is amazing what you can achieve.
6. Your subconscious is a great tool for creating change in your life once it is programmed for bigger thinking and enhanced performance.
7. The systematic reprogramming of the subconscious mind will yield infinite rewards.

8. It's time you take personal responsibility for where you are in life and take responsibility for changing your circumstances.

9. Thoughts of success and failure can never occupy the same space.

10. Your continuous thoughts and deliberate actions will determine your future.

11. When a negative thought comes to your mind, don't nurse it, don't rehearse it, just quickly disburse it.

12. There are things that you were born to do and things you were trained to do. The secret to success and fulfillment is to recognize the difference and be bold enough to not allow your training to deter you from doing what you were born to do.

13. Purpose inspires us to aim for powerful possibilities.

14. Navigating your way through life void of a sense of purpose is like sailing on the sea without a compass.

15. Your developed potential is the throttle that regulates the speed at which you begin to experience success and personal fulfillment.

16. The opinions of others should not influence you to doubt the words of the Creator of the universe.

17. True success is determined by assessing what you have done with your talents and abilities compared to what you were supposed to do with your talents and abilities.
18. Success without fulfillment of purpose is a formula for emptiness of the soul.
19. Your purpose is your divine assignment in life.
20. The ultimate impact of you fulfilling your purpose will be manifested in how you influence and impact individual lives in your sphere of influence and the society in which you live.
21. Your self-image is the battery cable to access the power of your potential.
22. Always strive to become more than you are, if you want to become all that you can be.
23. The sky is not the limit to your success, the moon, planets, sun, and stars await your arrival.
24. The contents of the seed determine its yield.
25. It is the internal transformation that will produce the external evidence of transformation.
26. It is time to experience the fullness of everything that has been encoded in you.

27. Don't diminish the value of your own skills or abilities and don't inflate the value of the skills or abilities of others.
28. Your yesterdays are not as important as your tomorrows.
29. Once you accept false debilitating statements as truth, they breed feelings of inferiority.
30. Low self-esteem, anger, and guilt are barriers to thinking bigger and achieving more.
31. The only limits you face are the limits you set in place.
32. Fear will snatch success from your hands in a split second.
33. Taking action minimizes fear.
34. The successful use failure as a stepping stone not a stumbling stone.
35. To achieve success you must stay focused and turn your defeats into victories.
36. The key to success is to stand boldly in the middle of your challenges and believe for success without wavering.
37. What a man believes in his mind, he achieves. What a man believes in his mind, he receives. What a man believes in his mind, controls his actions. What a man believes in his mind, directs his passions. What a man believes in his mind, becomes the rails that guide the train, on which he is the conductor.

38. Persistence is the most effective tool for maneuvering through resistance.

39. Your beliefs can light the path to success and empower you to travel to your destination. They can also render you powerless and disorientated in the darkness of mediocrity and failure.

40. On a daily basis tell yourself that you can do better and you deserve better.

41. It's time to leave the chickens alone and begin to soar with the eagles.

42. Maintaining the status quo or taking the easy route never leads to long-term success and peak performance.

43. Change is possible in any situation when the benefits of changing outweigh the need to remain the same.

44. To build my confidence I had to talk to myself. I would look in the mirror and say that what I have to impart is vitally important; people will pack auditoriums and convention halls to gain wisdom and insight from what I have to share. I'm not on an ego trip, but a divine mission to transform the lives of individuals and organizations.

45. To experience fulfillment, you must be free of any hindrances against maximizing your potential and discovering your destiny.

46. A positive attitude is an outward sign of the confidence within.

47. Kids who believe they can accomplish anything will accomplish anything.

48. Expectation creates an atmosphere of anticipation.

49. The world is teeming with people who practice sinking thinking.

50. For years I hung out with the chickens. I thought I was a chicken because I felt like a chicken. When I finally realized that I was an eagle, I packed my bags and said goodbye to my chicken friends in the barnyard. I have been soaring with the eagles ever since.

51. Make the most of your mind by making the most of your time.

52. No one can change your positive attitude into a negative attitude without your permission and assistance.

53. Everything around you is exerting influence on you daily, although you may not be aware of the cumulative effects.

54. Ordinary thinkers are a dime a dozen, creative thinkers are a rare find.

55. Your words and thoughts are the containers that carry your future.

56. If in your mind you allow garbage to creep, you will experience life on the garbage heap.

57. Attitudes and ambitions are transferable.

58. The strength of your "why" will determine how high you will fly.

59. Without a plan you cannot stand; without vision you will not complete the mission.

60. When you design the plan for your future, it is important to develop your vision or blueprint based on clear priorities.

61. True success is achieved when at the end of the day all those whose lives you have influenced have been enhanced by your success.

62. If you don't establish your priorities, others will establish them for you.

63. A vision without a method of implementation leads to great frustration.

64. Goals are your destination points on your way to fulfilling your destiny.

65. Don't confuse motion with progress.

66. Only speak the things you want even if you don't know how you are going to get them.

67. The mind does not know the difference between that which is imagined from that which is real.

68. Visualize your new reality on the screen of your vivid imagination.

69. You have to see it in your mind before you can see it with your eyes and touch it with your hands.

70. Knowledge is not power; acting on your knowledge produces power.

71. Whenever I make a decision to use my natural attributes, abilities, and ambitions to honor God, I activate the supernatural power, presence, and protection of God to help me achieve success.

72. You function according to the established laws of two realms, the natural realm and the supernatural or spirit realm.

73. The established laws of the supernatural or spiritual realm are more powerful and constant than the force of gravity.

74. The Master Creator waits for an invitation from His creation to assume His rightful place in a life.

75. The supernatural knowledge and power source from God enable you to accomplish what you could not accomplish with your own power, ability, influence, or intelligence.

76. It is not difficult to have faith in your future when the One who holds your future is by your side.

77. To experience a fruitful life you cannot be content as a human being. You must become a human doing. For it is the "doing" that maximizes the "being."

12 Powerful Affirmations for Transforming Your Life

1. Today and every day I take personal responsibility for believing, achieving and receiving the abundance that life has to offer.

2. Today and everyday I will use my talents, skills and experience to realize my full potential.

3. I will water my dreams and pull the weeds from around my ambitions so that my seeds of greatness produce a bountiful harvest in my life.

4. I am an original, I am one-of-a-kind and highly valued by God who has endowed me with special abilities and talents to fulfill my divine assignment.

5. I will always remember that on the other side of the mountains of my fears and failures is the green valley of my success.

6. I will restrict my mind to a diet of bountiful beliefs rich in positive possibilities, opulent opportunities and remarkable realities.

7. Today is the first day of the rest of my life. I am stepping out, moving up and not giving in. Look out world, here I come!

8. Today I will review my goals, revisit my plans, assess my progress, and keep moving forward.

9. I am better today than I was yesterday. I'll be better tomorrow than I am today and I have yet to give my best presentation.

10. I am building my new reality with the words that I speak and visions I see. My best is yet to come.

11. God I thank you that you are my constant companion on my journey through life. You are my source of power, ability, and influence.

12. The fruit of my thoughts, dreams and ambitions reach maturity through the actions of my hands; therefore I will never allow my hands to be idle.

Suggested Reading List

Each one of these classic books I am recommending is a book I have read and continue to revisit for inspiration, education and motivation.

Think and Grow Rich
Napoleon Hill
Fawcett Crest, Publisher

Mental Toughness for Success
Dr. I. V. Hilliard
Life Change Ministries
Houston, Texas

Understanding Your Potential
Dr. Myles Munroe
Destiny Image, Publisher

Releasing Your Potential
Dr. Myles Munroe
Destiny Image, Publisher

Attitude is Everything
Keith Harrell
HarperCollins, Publisher

The Magic of Thinking Big
David J Schwartz, PhD
Simon & Shuster, Publisher

For more information on the full offering of
Igniting the Power to Succeed™ workshops
keynote presentations, seminars, books, video tapes and services
presented by

T. R. Williams

contact

Eagles Wings Inc.
1749 Texas Parkway, Suite 180
Houston-Missouri City, Texas 77489
www.eagleswingsinc.com

To order individual or multiple copies of the book
Igniting the Power to Succeed

Call toll free
1-877-935-9955

$15.95
Plus $4.00 S&H
Major Credit Cards Accepted